The History of Canada

THE HISTORY OF CANADA

First edition. August 29, 2024.

Copyright © 2024 History Nerds.

ISBN: 979-8224231157

Written by History Nerds.

Also by History Nerds

Ancient Empires
The Ottoman Empire
Rome: The Rise and Fall
The Mongol Empire
The Assyrian Empire
Ancient Egypt

Celtic Heroes and Legends
Celtic History
William Butler Yeats: Nobel Prize Winning Poet
Robert the Bruce
Scáthach
Finn McCool
William Wallace: Scotland's Great Freedom Fighter

Frauen des Krieges
Boudica: Königin der Icener
Jeanne d'Arc
Irena Sendler
Virginia Hall

Königin Amanirenas
Anne Frank
Florence Nightingale
Nakano Takeko
Lyudmila Pawlitschenko
Lagertha

Geschichte der welt
Die Geschichte Schottlands
Die Geschichte von Wales

Great Wars of the World
World War 1
World War 2
The Napoleonic Wars: One Shot at Glory
The Serbian Revolution: 1804-1835
Peace Won by the Saber: The Crimean War, 1853-1856
The American Civil War

Pirate Chronicles
Grace O'Malley: The Pirate Queen of Ireland
Blackbeard
William Kidd
Ching Shih
Anne Bonny

The History of Ireland
The History of America
The History of Scotland
The History of Wales
The History of India
The History of Canada

Standalone
Grace O'Malley: Die Piratenkönigin von Irland

Table of Contents

Introduction

This book takes you on a journey through Canada's annals, from the ancient past to the vibrant, multicultural present.

We'll traverse a vast scope spanning millennia across a continent. Explore the ancient Indigenous cultures thriving long before European settlers arrived, living in perfect tune with the land's rhythms. Witness clashes and alliances between Indigenous peoples and newcomers, the forging of treaties, and colonialism's painful legacy. Trace the rise and fall of New France, the birth of the Dominion, and Canada's gradual evolution as a nation.

Along the way, meet fascinating characters - from intrepid explorers and visionary leaders to ordinary people facing the extraordinary. Stand with the coureurs des bois venturing into the wild to trade with the Haudenosaunee, navigating Indigenous diplomacy. March with soldiers on the Plains of Abraham, fight alongside Laura Secord in 1812, and join the rebels of Upper and Lower Canada struggling for responsible government. Witness Confederation's birth, the transcontinental railway's construction, and transformative waves of immigration.

This isn't just dry facts and dates - it's a vibrant human drama filled with courage and inspiration. Explore identity-shaping forces, from the English and French cultures' interplay to U.S. and Commonwealth influences. Confront dark chapters like Indigenous peoples' displacement and oppression and Japanese Canadian internment during WWII. And celebrate triumphant moments from women's suffrage to patriating the Constitution with the Charter of Rights and Freedoms.

Some view Canada's history as obligatory facts before the present. Others see it through preconceptions confirming existing beliefs. But to truly grasp Canada, we must grapple with complexities – not a simple narrative but a tapestry of conflicting stories and perspectives.

This book strives to offer a balanced, nuanced view drawing on the latest scholarship and amplifying marginalized voices. It shows Canada's history as a living, breathing entity reinterpreted through new evidence and evolving societal values.

Why does this matter? Canada's past echoes through generations, shaping society, politics, and culture today. Understanding the origins reveals future trajectories and our roles in molding destiny.

Whether a lifelong resident or newcomer, discover this fascinating story of resilience, adaptation, conflict, compromise, dreams realized and deferred - a story belonging to all who call Canada home and seek to understand its global place.

Together, let's embark across Canada's vast historical expanse, walking where others trod and imagining future paths. Marvel at the land's beauty, the diversity, and that enduring spirit forming a nation. For in the end, Canada's history isn't just events - it's a mirror reflecting ourselves and a compass guiding us forward.

Chapter 1: Dawn of the North: The Indigenous Peoples

A Timeline of Resilience

The history of the Indigenous peoples of Canada is a deeply rich and expansive tapestry, stretching back thousands of years before European contact. By around 6000 BC, as the glaciers receded, diverse Indigenous cultures had begun to emerge across the vast lands that would later become Canada. The ancestors of the Inuit, inhabiting the Arctic regions, developed technologies such as the kayak and igloo, adapting to the harsh northern climate. Meanwhile, in the Subarctic, Indigenous peoples led a nomadic lifestyle, following the seasonal movements of caribou, moose, and other game animals. As the landscape continued to evolve, so too did the Indigenous cultures that called it home.

Around 2000 BC, early agricultural practices began to take root in the Eastern Woodlands, particularly in the regions surrounding the Great Lakes and the St. Lawrence River. The cultivation of crops like corn, beans, and squash began to supplement the diets of these Indigenous peoples, who were already skilled hunters, fishers, and gatherers. This shift towards agriculture allowed for the growth of larger, more permanent settlements and set the stage for the development of complex societies in the centuries to come. In the coastal regions of what is now British Columbia, the peoples of the Plateau region combined fishing, hunting, and gathering to support their communities, with salmon becoming a staple of their diet.

By 1000 BC, distinct regional cultures had emerged across Canada. On the Pacific coast, the ancestors of the Coast Salish and other coastal peoples constructed large plank houses and began carving intricate totem poles, marking the development of a rich maritime culture. In the Great Lakes and St. Lawrence regions, the Woodland cultures began to rise, known for their burial mounds and the production of pottery. These early societies were not isolated; they engaged in long-distance trade, exchanging goods like copper, shells, and obsidian, indicating a high level of social organization and interaction with distant regions.

As time progressed into the Archaic period, between 1000 BC and 500 AD, Indigenous cultures across Canada became increasingly sophisticated. On the Plains, Indigenous peoples, such as the ancestors of the Blackfoot, Cree, and Assiniboine, honed their skills in bison hunting, a practice that would later become central to their way of life. The introduction of the bow and arrow around this time increased the efficiency of hunting and warfare, further shaping the social and political dynamics of Plains cultures.

In the Eastern Woodlands, the early agricultural practices continued to evolve, leading to the rise of more complex societies. The Hopewell culture, flourishing between 100 BC and 500 AD in the Ohio River Valley, exerted influence on neighboring regions, including southern Ontario. These peoples constructed elaborate earthworks and engaged in long-distance trade networks that spanned much of North America. It was during this period that the ancestors of the Haudenosaunee (Iroquois) began to establish themselves in the Great Lakes region, building longhouses and developing a matrilineal society, where lineage and inheritance were traced through the mother.

As the centuries unfolded, the Late Woodland period, which began around 500-1000 AD, saw Indigenous cultures across Canada thriving in diverse environments. In the Arctic, the Inuit culture had fully developed, with advanced hunting and fishing techniques that allowed them to thrive in their challenging surroundings. Meanwhile, in the Eastern Woodlands, the Haudenosaunee Confederacy, or Iroquois League, began to take shape. This powerful alliance of five (later six) nations would become one of the most influential Indigenous political entities in North America. The Confederacy brought peace among its member nations and created a system of governance based on collective decision-making.

On the Great Plains, Indigenous peoples continued to rely on bison hunting, and their societies became increasingly complex, with bands organized under the leadership of chiefs and councils of elders. In the Northwest Coast region, Indigenous cultures like the Tlingit, Haida, and Coast Salish developed intricate social hierarchies, with chiefs, nobles, and commoners. The potlatch, a ceremonial feast where wealth was redistributed among the community, became central to their social and political life.

By 1000 AD, the Mississippian culture, centered in the southeastern United States, began to influence Indigenous peoples in southern Ontario. The Mississippians were known for their large, complex societies, mound-building, and extensive trade networks. In southern Ontario, the Neutral, Huron-Wendat, and Petun nations developed large fortified villages and engaged in agriculture, particularly the cultivation of corn, beans, and squash. These societies were highly organized, with complex political systems and long-distance trade connections that extended far beyond their immediate regions.

Around 1300 AD, the Haudenosaunee Confederacy began to solidify, with the creation of the Great Law of Peace, a constitution that governed the alliance. Founded by the Peacemaker and his spokesperson, Hiawatha, the Confederacy brought an end to inter-tribal warfare among the member nations and established a powerful political structure that would shape the history of the region for centuries to come.

By the 15th century, Indigenous trade networks spanned much of North America, facilitating the exchange of goods, cultures, and ideas. Birchbark canoes, a technological innovation of the Algonquian-speaking peoples of the Eastern Woodlands, became widely used by many Indigenous groups for transportation and trade. These extensive trade routes connected the peoples of Canada to distant regions, creating a vibrant network of cultural exchange.

On the eve of European contact, the Indigenous peoples of Canada were thriving in a vast array of environments. The population of what is now Canada is estimated to have been between 500,000 and 2 million people, organized into hundreds of nations, each with its own language, culture, and governance system. In the Arctic, the Inuit were expert hunters and fishers, relying on whales, seals, and fish for sustenance. Their society was organized into small, family-based groups that traveled seasonally in search of resources.

In the Subarctic, the Dene, Cree, and Innu peoples lived as semi-nomadic hunter-gatherers, moving with the seasons to follow game like caribou and moose. On the Great Plains, the Blackfoot, Cree, and other nations were skilled bison hunters, using their resources efficiently and organizing their societies into bands, each led by a chief and council of elders. The Eastern Woodlands were dominated by the Haudenosaunee Confederacy, a powerful alliance that balanced the autonomy of individual nations with the need for collective decision-making. Meanwhile, on the Northwest Coast, Indigenous nations like the Haida, Tlingit, and Coast Salish were skilled artisans, creating intricate carvings, totem poles, and woven textiles. Their societies were hierarchical, with powerful chiefs and elaborate social ceremonies, such as the potlatch, marking their social and political life.

Although contact with Europeans would bring dramatic changes, it is important to recognize that the arrival of European settlers was not the first instance of external influence. Around 1000 AD, Norse explorers from Greenland, led by Leif Erikson, established a settlement at L'Anse aux Meadows in Newfoundland, marking the first known European contact with the Indigenous peoples of Canada. However, this contact was brief and did not lead to lasting interactions or settlements. The Norse encountered the Indigenous peoples they referred to as "Skraelings," likely the ancestors of the Beothuk, but conflicts and the harsh environment led the Norse to abandon their settlement after only a few years.

It wasn't until the late 15th century that European exploration began in earnest, driven by the desire for new trade routes and resources. By this time, Indigenous societies across Canada were well-established, diverse, and thriving, each uniquely adapted to the land and environment they inhabited. As European explorers ventured across the Atlantic, they would encounter these resilient and complex cultures, forever altering the course of history for both the Indigenous peoples of Canada and the newcomers from across the sea.

Survival and Adaptation: The Inuit Way

The vast Arctic expanse, with subzero temperatures, icy winds, and months of perpetual darkness, is home to the remarkable Inuit people. For millennia, they have not just survived but thrived in one of Earth's harshest environments. Their ability to adapt showcases ingenuity, resilience, and profound natural world understanding.

The Inuit, meaning "the people" in Inuktitut, have inhabited Arctic regions of Canada, Greenland, and Alaska for thousands of years. They descended from the Thule people who migrated eastward across the Arctic around 1000 AD. The Inuit developed a rich culture and deep environmental knowledge passed down orally over generations.

Their primary challenge was the Arctic's extreme cold and resource scarcity. Winter temperatures plummet to -50°C (-58°F), and snow and ice cover the landscape most of the year. No trees grow, and vegetation is limited to low shrubs, mosses, and lichens. To survive this unforgiving setting, the Inuit learned resourcefulness and creativity from the limited avvailable materials.

The igloo exemplifies remarkable Inuit ingenuity. This dome-shaped snow shelter marvelously combines engineering with deep snow and ice property understanding. Constructing an igloo starts by finding a suitable spot with deep, compact snow. Long snow knives cut snow blocks about 1 meter (3 feet) long and 15 centimeters (6 inches) thick. These blocks get stacked spirally, angling inward slightly to create the dome. Loose snow fills gaps and hardens like mortar.

The igloo's design masterfully insulates and ventilates. Trapped air between snow blocks insulates, keeping the interior warm. A small top hole lets cold air escape and fresh air enter, preventing carbon dioxide buildup. The entrance typically sits below the main level, creating a cold trap to stop warm air from escaping. With a small fire or oil lamp inside, an igloo can reach 20°C (68°F) warmer than outside.

The kayak is another amazing Inuit innovation - a narrow, lightweight boat made from driftwood or whalebone covered in seal or caribou skin. Designed for Arctic water hunting and travel, it navigates ice floes swiftly and maneuverably. The Inuit use double-bladed paddles skillfully to propel kayaks long distances, even in rough seas, silently sneaking up on prey like seals, walruses and whales. Hunting tools like harpoons, lances and inflated seal skin floats equip the kayaks. When an animal gets harpooned, the float stops it from sinking so hunters can retrieve it.

But Inuit survival goes beyond shelter and transport. They developed deep knowledge about local plants and animals, using them comprehensively for food, clothing and tools. They hunt caribou, musk oxen, polar bears, seals, walruses and whales, utilizing every part - eating the meat, making clothes and tents from skins, crafting tools and weapons from bones, and using fat for fuel and light. They also gather berries, roots and seaweed to supplement diets.

Behind Inuit Arctic survival is more than skills - their strong social bonds and cultural values play a key role. They deeply respect nature and believe animals have spirits deserving honor. Resources are shared, with everyone working together for the common good of community survival.

The igloo and kayak represent just two remarkable examples of Inuit ingenuity adapting to a harsh setting. They reflect not just practical skills, but a cultural worldview of respecting and living in balance with the natural world. In our changing world facing environmental challenges, the Inuit offer inspiration for living lighter on Earth through sustainability and environmental harmony.

Chapter 2: European Exploration

Why Brave the Unknown?

What drives humans to explore the unknown and venture into uncharted territories? From our earliest days, an innate curiosity and thirst for discovery have propelled us. But what compels some individuals to take that curiosity to the extreme? They risk everything - comfort, safety, even life itself - to seek new lands and experiences.

Throughout history, explorers journeyed across oceans, through jungles, and over mountains, driven by a web of motivations. Their voyages expanded our understanding of the world and our place in it, but they also came at immense cost. To truly grasp the heart of exploration, we must examine the forces that propelled these adventurers forward.

For some, the allure was the promise of glory and fame. Before mass media, when heroes were few, explorers like Columbus, da Gama, and Magellan captured public imagination. Their names etched in history's annals, the prospect of such enduring renown motivated ambitious individuals to undertake daring feats.

Others sought wealth and power. European nations raced to claim new territories, trade routes, and resources during the Age of Exploration. Explorers who could deliver these prizes gained immense personal fortune and political influence. The promise of riches - whether gold, spices, or land - lured adventurers to brave the unknown's perils.

Yet, not all were driven by self-interest. Many were genuinely curious about the world beyond borders, eager to fill blank spaces on maps and learn about other cultures. For them, exploration nobilized the pursuit of expanding human knowledge. They endured hardship for the sake of discovery, seeing themselves as servants of science and progress.

It's tempting to romanticize explorers as heroic figures with pure ideals. But reality was messier. As products of their societies, they carried cultural superiority, religious zeal, and imperialist ambition. Indigenous peoples stewarding lands for generations developed rich, environment-adapted cultures. But to explorers, they were often primitives, obstacles or resources to exploit. This mindset devastated native populations through disease, violence, and lifestyle disruption.

How can we interpret explorers' complex motivations? We must recognize their humanity - both strengths and flaws. Their values and beliefs shaped them, even as their journeys shaped history. Some seeked noble ends; others, base desires. Most blended both, with evolving motives.

We must also contextualize their era. During the Age of Exploration, feudalism gave way to capitalism, science challenged dogma, and technologies eased long travel. Explorers reflected and catalyzed these transformations, their voyages reflecting and altering history's course.

Explorers' motives spanned the human experience: glory, wealth, knowledge, duty, restlessness, adventure... But all dared the unknown, risking all for discovery's sake.

As we continue our journey through the Age of Exploration, let's familiarize ourselves with three key terms that will give us a solid foundation to appreciate the significance and context of the stories that defined this period.

The first is the caravel, a small, highly maneuverable sailing ship that revolutionized navigation. Don't underestimate its size; this unassuming vessel was a game-changer. Its sleek design and advanced rigging allowed explorers to navigate treacherous waters and uncharted territories with ease. The caravel symbolized human ingenuity and an unrelenting pursuit of discovery.

Originating from the Arabic word "qārib" meaning "skiff," the Portuguese developed the caravel in the 15th century. Its design combined European and Arab shipbuilding techniques, creating a vessel perfect for exploration. Caravels typically had two or three masts with lateen sails that enabled sailing close to the wind, ideal for coastlines and against the wind. Their shallow draft allowed river and shallow water exploration, while sturdy construction withstood long ocean voyages. Speed, agility, and seaworthiness made the caravel the choice for famous explorers like Christopher Columbus and Vasco da Gama. Its development was crucial to Portuguese and Spanish exploration success, allowing them to establish global trade routes and colonial empires. The caravel's legacy influenced shipbuilding for centuries and shaped the modern world.

Another tool was the astrolabe a device that some may mistake for a fancy paperweight, but this ancient astronomical tool unlocked celestial navigation secrets. By measuring celestial body positions, explorers could precisely determine latitude and chart their course. The astrolabe represented human ingenuity and our enduring fascination with the stars.

With origins dating to ancient Greece, the sophisticated astrolabe played a vital navigation role during the Age of Exploration. It consisted of a disk with a rotating alidade (sighting device) and engraved scales that allowed navigators to measure celestial body altitudes above the horizon. By observing the sun or stars at known times, explorers could determine their crucial latitude for charting vast ocean courses. The astrolabe evolved over centuries, incorporating knowledge from Greek, Islamic, and European astronomers and mathematicians. Using it required deep astronomy and mathematics understanding, making it essential for skilled navigators. Providing accurate latitude was a game-changer, enabling explorers to venture farther from shore and chart new trade routes confidently. The astrolabe's legacy extends beyond navigation; its design and principles influenced other scientific instruments and laid the foundation for modern techniques.

Third is circumnavigation. To circumnavigate means to sail around the world - a feat once deemed impossible until Ferdinand Magellan's expedition proved otherwise. Circumnavigation is no easy task; it requires skill, determination, and luck. But those who achieve this monumental undertaking forever alter our world understanding and sense of place in it.

Most did not accept the Earth's spherical shape, viewing vast oceans as impenetrable barriers filled with untold dangers. Ferdinand Magellan's expedition (1519-1522) made circumnavigation a reality. Though Magellan himself did not finish as he was killed in the Philippines, Juan Sebastián Elcano's crew completed the journey after his death, definitively proving the world was round. This groundbreaking achievement opened new trade routes, colonial opportunities, and fundamentally changed humanity's world perception. Circumnavigation required immense skill, courage, and perseverance as navigators battled treacherous weather, uncharted waters, disease, and starvation. Magellan's success testified to human resilience and the indomitable exploration spirit. Today, circumnavigation remains remarkable, but technology aids navigation, making it more accessible for sailors, aviators, and solo adventurers continuing to push boundaries in innovative ways. Circumnavigation's legacy shapes world understanding, fosters global trade and cultural exchange, and inspires generations to pursue possibilities.

Caravel, astrolabe, and circumnavigate - more than words, they form the building blocks of the Age of Exploration. Understanding their meaning and significance helps us piece together the explorers' incredible stories who ventured into the unknown. As we embark on this pivotal era in human history, keep these terms in mind as our compass, guiding us through triumphs, tragedies, discoveries, and disasters that shaped our world.

Vikings in the New World

In a clash of cultures over a thousand years ago, the Vikings' brief journey to North America marked the first known European encounter with the New World - a harbinger of a new era.

The story centers around the Eriksson family. Erik the Red founded the first Norse settlement in Greenland around 985 AD after being exiled from Iceland. His son Leif, an ambitious and skilled navigator, pushed the boundaries of Norse exploration even further.

Leif didn't plan to reach North America. According to the Icelandic Sagas - oral histories written down centuries later - he was tasked with bringing Christianity to Greenland around 1000 AD. On his return voyage from Norway, his ship blew off course. He inadvertently discovered a land west of Greenland, naming it Vinland for the wild grapes growing there.

Intrigued, Leif mounted an expedition with a crew of 35 in a knorr - a Viking longship suited for ocean voyages. They established a small settlement called Leifsbudir, likely in present-day Newfoundland, Canada.

Leifsbudir served as a base for further exploration and a way-station between Greenland and Vinland. The Norse found the land rich in resources like timber, game, fish, and pastures for livestock. However, they encountered the indigenous peoples of the region, whom they called Skraelings.

Interactions between the groups involved trade and conflict. The Sagas recount trades of red cloth for furs, but also skirmishes and killings on both sides. Leif's brother Thorvald was killed in one encounter, and the settlement felt increasingly threatened.

Despite its promising start, the Vinland colony was abandoned within a decade due to the threat of attacks, the challenges of sustaining a remote community, and internal disputes. The dream of a permanent Norse presence in North America faded into legend.

The Norse left little archaeological trace until the 1960s, when excavations at L'Anse aux Meadows in Newfoundland uncovered a Viking outpost, confirming the Sagas. The site, now a UNESCO World Heritage Site, features reconstructed sod buildings and artifacts that bring the Viking experience to life.

Leif Eriksson's legacy extends beyond the fleeting settlement. The Vikings proved transatlantic voyages were possible, paving the way for later European exploration and colonization. While Columbus is often credited with "discovering" the Americas, Leif beat him by nearly 500 years.

However, the Viking voyages had little lasting impact. Unlike later European powers, they lacked the technology, population pressure, and incentives for sustained colonization. Their presence remained a historical footnote until the 19th century, when Scandinavian immigrants celebrated the sagas as a source of pride in the United States.

Leif's story reminds us that history is full of might-have-beens and forgotten firsts. We can consider alternate timelines where the Norse maintained a North American presence, with profound implications. It also underscores the challenges of sustaining remote settlements - a lesson later colonists would relearn.

As we explore the Age of Exploration, the Viking voyages to Vinland serve as a prologue, hinting at the discoveries and encounters to come. They remind us that the world was wider and more interconnected than medieval Europeans imagined. Leif Eriksson and his crew were the first Europeans to glimpse the shores of the New World, but far from the last.

Columbus and Cabot: A Tale of Two Journeys

The history of exploration is illuminated by two brilliant names - Christopher Columbus and John Cabot. These daring navigators sailed under rival nations but shared one dream - finding a western passage to

Asia's riches. However, their journeys led them to a New World, forever altering history's course.

Columbus, an Italian sailing for Spain, and Cabot, a Venetian exploring for England, embodied the spirit of the Age of Discovery. They were ambitious visionaries, driven by a thirst for knowledge, glory, and wealth. At a time when most believed the world ended at the horizon, they dared venture beyond the map's edge.

To grasp the significance of their voyages, we must compare and contrast their motivations, experiences, and legacies. What drove them to risk everything for the unknown? How did their discoveries shape Europe's worldview? And why do we remember Columbus as the discoverer of America while Cabot faded into relative obscurity?

Both explorers sought to revolutionize trade by finding a direct route to the East's spice markets. Columbus convinced Spain's monarchs to finance his expedition, promising a shortcut to India across the Atlantic. Meanwhile, Cabot aimed to one-up his rival by finding an even shorter northern route with English merchants' backing.

In 1492, Columbus set sail with three ships - the Niña, Pinta, and Santa Maria. After a perilous journey, he landed in the Bahamas, believing he had reached Asia's outer islands. Over four voyages, he explored the Caribbean, establishing Spain's claim to the New World.

Five years later, in 1497, Cabot embarked with a single ship, the Matthew. He reached North America's coast - likely Newfoundland or Labrador - and explored the region, claiming it for England. Like Columbus, he thought he had found a new route to Asia.

Both men encountered indigenous peoples, but their interactions differed. Columbus saw potential for trade, Christian conversion, and exploitation. His voyages initiated the Columbian Exchange, transferring crops, animals, and diseases that transformed both sides of the Atlantic, often devastating Native Americans.

Cabot's encounter was briefer and less consequential. He traded with indigenous people and noted the rich fishing grounds off the coast. His voyage laid the foundation for later English claims in North America and the lucrative cod fisheries of the Grand Banks.

But their voyages revealed a startling truth - they had not reached Asia but lands previously unknown to Europeans. The idea of a New World separate from Asia gradually took hold, revolutionizing geography, trade, and geopolitics. Spain, England, and other European powers raced to claim and colonize these new territories.

Columbus and Cabot opened the floodgates for a wave of exploration, exploitation, and settlement that transformed the Americas and had global repercussions. Their journeys marked the beginning of the Columbian Era, a period of European dominance and colonialism that reshaped the world for centuries.

Yet their legacies diverged. Columbus became an icon - the daring discoverer who defied skeptics and transformed human history, for better or worse. His name graces countless places and monuments across the Americas. Cabot, while significant, became a historical footnote, overshadowed by his more famous counterpart.

This disparity reflects historical memory's vagaries and the politics of commemoration. Spain promoted Columbus as a national hero, while England's colonial attentions shifted elsewhere. The scope and impact of Columbus's four voyages dwarfed Cabot's single journey. And the United States, as a rising power, found in Columbus an origin story and symbol of the spirit of discovery.

Today, both men's legacies are subject to reexamination. Greater scrutiny is given to Columbus's impact on Native Americans, with some calling for a reckoning with the darker aspects of his legacy. Cabot, in turn, has been embraced by some as a neglected figure in the story of Atlantic exploration.

In comparing these two explorers, we see individual actions' indelible imprint on history's course. Columbus and Cabot were products of their time, driven by their age's ambitions and assumptions. Their voyages reflect the best and worst of the European Age of Discovery - the thirst for knowledge and conquest, the wonder of exploration and the devastation of exploitation.

For all their flaws and failings, Columbus and Cabot were pioneers who dared to dream beyond their world's limits. Their voyages marked a turning point in human history, setting in motion a process of encounter, exchange, and transformation that continues today. In our age of globalization, their stories still resonate - as cautionary tales, as inspiration for exploration, and as reminders of our interconnected world.

Confronting the Atlantic

For centuries, the vast Atlantic Ocean spanning over 41 million square miles challenged and daunted explorers and adventurers. Its immense expanse, erratic weather, and dangerous currents tested even the most skilled navigators. Crossing this ocean demanded immense courage, innovation, and grit.

One primary issue plagued early seafarers attempting Atlantic voyages – the ocean's sheer scale. With no land in sight for weeks or months, sailors relied on their navigation abilities, limited supplies, and sturdy vessels to survive. Mapping accurate courses proved difficult without precise tools and maps, often causing ships to go off-track and become lost.

The Atlantic is notorious for violent storms and hurricanes that can rapidly turn a smooth voyage life-threatening. Towering waves, powerful winds, and torrential rains easily capsized ships or inflicted significant damage, leaving crews helpless against nature's fury. Without modern forecasting, sailors had little warning of looming storms and depended on instincts and experience.

Understanding ocean currents proved another daunting challenge. Major currents like the Gulf Stream greatly influence a ship's speed and direction. Unaware of these currents or miscalculating their effects, explorers frequently veered drastically off course, adding weeks or months to journeys.

Consequences of failing these challenges were grim. Lost ships or those caught in storms quickly depleted food and water, leading to widespread illness and death. Scurvy from vitamin C deficiency decimated entire crews on extended voyages. Desperation and hardship sometimes incited mutinies as sailors turned on captains and each other for survival.

Yet daring explorers and innovators confronted and overcame Atlantic crossing difficulties. Developing better navigation tools like the sextant allowed accurate latitude readings from the sun and stars. Precise timekeeping devices enabled longitude calculations for accurate maps.

Improved ship designs also proved vital. The 15th century caravel's light, maneuverable design with triangular lateen sails helped coastal navigation and sailing against winds. Copper sheathing and stronger hull materials later protected ships from barnacles, shipworms, and rigors of ocean travel.

To combat disease and malnutrition, some captains preserved variety in crews' diets. Introducing citrus fruits, sauerkraut and foods rich in vitamin C prevented scurvy. Better food storage and rationing extended limited supplies.

Groundbreaking voyages like Christopher Columbus's 1492 Atlantic crossing and Magellan's 1522 circumnavigation highlight these solutions' success. These opened new trade routes, economic growth, and expanded world geographic understanding.

While imperfect with remaining challenges, early explorers' solutions built a foundation for future maritime advances. Today's technology, forecasting, and global positioning make Atlantic crossings relatively routine. However, we remember those pioneers' bravery, ingenuity, and sacrifices in confronting the Atlantic, paving our modern, interconnected world.

A Timeline of Discovery

It's hard to overstate how much the Age of Exploration impacted human history. To truly appreciate it, we should follow a timeline of pivotal expeditions that forever altered our world. This remarkable journey shows how an insatiable human curiosity, evolving technologies, and economic ambitions drove the relentless pursuit of knowledge and new horizons. It connected continents and cultures in unprecedented ways.

As previously mentioned the earliest European explorers were the Vikings, fierce Scandinavian seafarers. Around 985 AD, Erik the Red discovered Greenland and established a settlement., around 1000 AD, his son Leif Erikson reached North American shores at a place called Vinland (likely Newfoundland), becoming the first known European to set foot there - centuries before Columbus.

However, the Viking expeditions were isolated events. Sustained contact between Europe and the Americas required advancements in maritime technology and shifts in economic and political forces. This sparked the true era of exploration:

• In 1415, the Portuguese captured Ceuta, marking their empire's beginning.• In 1488, Bartolomeu Dias rounded southern Africa, opening an Asian trade route.• In 1492, Christopher Columbus, sponsored by Spain, made his first voyage to the Bahamas.• In 1497, John Cabot explored Newfoundland's coast under the English flag.• In 1498, Vasco da Gama reached India via the Cape of Good Hope, establishing a direct trade route.• In 1500, Pedro Álvares Cabral claimed Brazil for Portugal.• In 1513, Vasco Núñez de Balboa crossed the Isthmus of Panama and sighted the Pacific Ocean.• Between 1519-1522, Ferdinand Magellan's expedition completed the first global circumnavigation.• In 1534, Jacques Cartier explored the Gulf of Saint Lawrence, claiming Canada for France.

Each expedition expanded the known world, setting the stage for colonization and far-reaching cultural, economic, and political impacts. The Columbian Exchange transferred crops, diseases, and populations between the Old and New Worlds, dramatically reshaping global demographics and agriculture.

European powers raced to claim new territories. The Portuguese built trade posts along African, Indian, and Asian coasts. Spain focused on the Americas, where Hernán Cortés overthrew the Aztec Empire (1519-1521) and Francisco Pizarro conquered the Incas (1532-1572). England, France, and the Dutch also competed for colonies and trade routes.

Controversies and conflicts arose. The 1494 Treaty of Tordesillas divided the New World between Spain and Portugal, but other nations largely ignored its Line of Demarcation. Disputes over territories and trade escalated into wars and shifting alliances.

Indigenous populations suffered profoundly. The arrival of Europeans brought diseases they had no immunity to, decimating their numbers. Colonization often exploited natives through forced labor and suppressed their cultures and practices.

In reflecting on this era, we need nuance - acknowledging both the triumphs of human ingenuity and the tragic consequences of colonization. The courage to venture into the unknown expanded our world's understanding, but also laid bare human cruelty's depths and cultural clashes' devastating impact.

The Age of Exploration's legacy still shapes our interconnected global society with its complex web of international relations, trade routes, and cultural exchanges. It forever changed human history's course, setting the stage for the modern world. As we navigate today's globalized challenges and opportunities, we must learn from this era's successes and failures to build a more equitable, sustainable future.

The Legacy of Exploration

European exploration left an indelible, transformative mark on North America that still reverberates today. From decimating indigenous populations to introducing new agricultural practices, the effects were sweeping and far-reaching.

One of the most striking pieces of evidence is the devastating toll of European diseases on Native American peoples. A Quaternary Science Reviews study estimates that before European contact, around 60 million indigenous people lived in the Americas. By 1600, that number had plummeted to just 5-6 million. The researchers point to introduced diseases like smallpox, measles, and influenza as the primary cause - diseases the native populations had never encountered and had no immunity against. Some scholars argue the population estimates are too high, but even conservative figures show a catastrophic decline of at least 50% from European disease.

But the devastation went far beyond demographics. Historian David J. Weber notes in "The Spanish Frontier in North America" that Spanish conquistadors and missionaries aimed not just to claim land, but forcibly convert indigenous people to Christianity. This often brutally suppressed native beliefs and imposed European culture.

Archaeological sites across the Southwest and California show the cultural disruption vividly. Native burial practices shifted to Christian styles. Indigenous buildings gave way to European-style structures. Yet as anthropologist Louise Burkhart argues in "The Slippery Earth," indigenous peoples also adapted and blended Christian beliefs into syncretic new cultural forms that still exist today.

The economic impacts were equally transformative. Elinor Melville's "A Plague of Sheep" documents how introducing European livestock led to overgrazing, soil erosion, and displacing native species. But as Alfred Crosby writes in "The Columbian Exchange," foods like potatoes, tomatoes and maize also revolutionized agriculture globally in an ecological exchange between Old and New Worlds.

Darkest of all were the exploitation and oppression that followed. The brutal transatlantic slave trade forcibly transported millions of Africans to work plantations and mines - a direct result of colonization. And the displacement and mistreatment of indigenous peoples, often justified by racist notions, left deep wounds. The Trail of Tears was just one injustice in removing tribes from ancestral lands.

These traumas shape society still today. As Eduardo Bonilla-Silva argues in "Racism without Racists," the legacy of colonization and slavery underlies ongoing racial inequalities and tensions in the United States.

The evidence clearly shows the profound, lasting impacts of European exploration in reshaping North America - demographically, culturally, economically, and ecologically. But we must view it with nuance, not simple triumph or victimhood narratives. Cultural exchange and adaptation coexisted with brutal exploitation.

As we reckon with this legacy, an honest, evidence-based understanding is vital. It allows us to confront painful truths, recognize colonization's ongoing effects, and work towards a more equitable future. By learning from both the triumphs and tragedies, we can chart a path that honors the resilience and contributions of all who shaped North American history.

Chapter 3: Fur, Faith, and the Fight for the Frontier

Who Held the Reins of the Fur Trade?

The provocative question of who truly controlled the fur trade cuts to the heart of a complex era that shaped Canada's foundations. It invites us to peel back layers of history and examine the intricate web of alliances, rivalries, and power struggles that defined the fur trade. As we'll see, the answer is not simple.

We must first appreciate the fur trade's immense importance in Canadian history. For centuries, it drove European exploration, settlement, and economic development in what became Canada. The fur trade drew European powers deep into the continent's heart, where vast networks of Indigenous nations had traded furs long before Europeans arrived.

At first glance, European powers with superior technology and insatiable fur demand seemed to hold all the cards. After all, they controlled ships that carried furs to Europe, guns that gave military superiority, and manufactured goods that Indigenous peoples depended on. But this view overlooks Indigenous groups' critical role.

Indigenous peoples were not passive participants. They actively and shrewdly negotiated, using the fur trade to their advantage. They played European rivals against each other, forging strategic alliances that shifted power balances in their favor. They controlled access to the interior and acted as essential middlemen and guides. Fiercely, they resisted European attempts to impose control over their lands and way of life.

One misconception is that Europeans simply exploited Indigenous peoples in the fur trade. While exploitation and cultural disruption occurred, reality was more nuanced. Many Indigenous groups saw opportunities to acquire new goods, technologies, and allies that strengthened their positions. They engaged in trade on their terms, often dictating exchange terms and walking away if unsatisfied.

Another misconception is that a single European power or company like the Hudson's Bay Company controlled the fur trade. In reality, it involved multiple competitive players with their own agendas. The French, English, Dutch, and Spanish all vied for dominance, forming alliances and waging wars with far-reaching Indigenous consequences.

To truly understand who controlled the fur trade, we need a holistic, nuanced perspective that accounts for Indigenous peoples' agency and resilience. We must look beyond simple European dominance narratives and recognize the complex economic, political, and cultural forces at play.

Consider the Haudenosaunee (Iroquois) Confederacy, a powerful northeastern Indigenous alliance. The Haudenosaunee were master diplomats who expanded power and influence through the fur trade. They played the French and English against each other, extracting concessions and building alliances to maintain independence and their way of life.

The Haudenosaunee were not alone in this strategy. The Wendat (Huron), Anishinaabeg (Ojibwe), Cree, and many others used the fur trade to their advantage. They adapted to new technologies and economic opportunities while fiercely defending autonomy and cultural traditions. They developed sophisticated, vast trading networks that challenged European control and ownership notions.

This does not mean Indigenous peoples were unaffected. The influx of European goods and diseases profoundly impacted societies, disrupting traditional life and creating dependencies. Some faced near-extinction from disease and warfare. Others relocated or adapted to new economic and political realities.

Despite challenges, Indigenous peoples remained vital fur trade forces, shaping contours and outcomes Europeans could not fully control. They navigated a complex, changing world with skill, resilience, and determination as active agents, not passive victims.

In short, no single group controlled the fur trade. It involved multiple actors with interests and strategies. European powers depended on Indigenous peoples for furs, land knowledge, and military alliances, despite technological advantages.

Indigenous peoples were diverse and adaptable, not monolithic or helpless. They used the fur trade advantageously, building alliances, acquiring goods and technologies, and maintaining cultural traditions amidst immense change. Often, they resisted or subverted European control attempts, asserting agency and autonomy.

To grasp the fur trade's complexities, we must move beyond simplistic European dominance and Indigenous victimhood narratives. We must recognize Indigenous resilience, competing European interests, and how the fur trade profoundly transformed North America's social, economic, and political landscape.

Asking who controlled the fur trade opens new inquiry and understanding avenues. We begin seeing it not as one-sided exploitation and conquest, but as a dynamic system shaping Canada's foundations. We appreciate Indigenous peoples' incredible resilience and adaptability in skillfully navigating and leaving an indelible mark.

Unraveling the Complex Web

To truly understand Canada's fur trade era, we need to explore the intricate web of alliances, rivalries, and the role of the Métis Nation. These weren't just footnotes in history - they formed the very fabric of how Canada developed. By grasping their origins, meanings, and vital influence, we can appreciate the rich yet tumultuous narrative of this pivotal period.

Alliances acted as the lifeblood pumping through the fur trade's veins. Envision a grand chessboard where Indigenous nations and European powers strategically partnered up, each move calculated to serve diplomacy and self-interest. Forging alliances unlocked access to vast trading networks, military aid, and maintained a delicate power balance across the ever-shifting landscape.

While alliances bound the fur trade together, rivalries threatened to slice through and unravel it. This lucrative business bred cutthroat competition as European powers vied for control, often dragging Indigenous allies into conflicts.

The bitter French-English rivalry endured over a century of wars, intrigue, and economic clashes as they battled for dominance across the continent. France allied with the Huron-Wendat and Algonquin while England linked with the Haudenosaunee. Yet Indigenous nations also stoked complex inter-tribal rivalries, sometimes exacerbated by European trade interests.

Shaped by this cultural collision, the Métis Nation emerged as a distinct Indigenous people born of the fur trade crucible. They forged a unique identity blending European and Indigenous traditions like Cree, Ojibwe and Saulteaux cultures. The Métis became renowned mediators skilled at hunting, trapping, and navigating between both worlds.

Far from passive bystanders, the Métis played active roles driving the fur trade's course and asserting their rights under leaders like Cuthbert Grant and Louis Riel. Their story epitomizes the profound exchanges sparked by the trade, making the Métis narrative integral to understanding this era.

The Rise of the Métis Nation

The Métis Nation emerged as a distinct and resilient people during the fur trade era in Canada. This era saw a collision and fusion of

Indigenous and European cultures. Our study zooms in on the birth of the Métis and explores how they navigated the frontier's complexities.

The story unfolds across the vast Northwest, where the fur trade's reach extended deep into the continent's heart. The Cree, Ojibwe, and Saulteaux Indigenous peoples inhabited these lands for a long time. They developed rich cultures and trade networks. As Britain and France pushed westward in the 1700s, driven by the lucrative fur trade, they formed alliances and rivalries with various Indigenous nations.

Into this intricate web stepped the Métis, born from unions between European fur traders and Indigenous women. These strategic marriage alliances gave rise to a new bicultural population. The Métis inherited knowledge and skills from both worlds. They learned Indigenous expertise in hunting, trapping, and navigating the land. They also gained European acumen in trade and diplomacy.

The Métis faced the challenge of carving out their place in a rapidly shifting landscape. They were neither fully European nor Indigenous, straddling two often-tense worlds. Yet this challenge became their strength. The Métis developed a distinct identity, language (Michif), and way of life drawing from both maternal and paternal lineages.

To navigate the fur trade's complexities, the Métis employed key strategies: 1. They became skilled middlemen, using their bicultural heritage to facilitate trade between Indigenous nations and Europeans. Their ability to move between worlds made them indispensable. 2. They formed their own trade networks and economic enterprises, like the famous Red River cart brigades. By the early 1800s, they ran a thriving pemmican trade to fuel the fur trade. 3. They asserted political autonomy, resisting colonial powers' attempts to control them. Under leaders like Cuthbert Grant and Louis Riel, they fought for rights and lands.

The Métis' strategies had significant outcomes. They became a major fur trade force, with communities like Red River (now Winnipeg) as economic and political hubs. By the mid-1800s, the

Métis Nation numbered tens of thousands with a distinct culture and nationhood.

However, their success brought conflict with the expanding Canadian state seeking control over the west. Though defeated militarily, the Métis' resistance forced Canada to recognize them as a distinct Indigenous people with land and self-determination rights – a struggle continuing today.

The Métis Nation's rise teaches us about cultural exchange's power and adaptation amid adversity. They could have been marginalized by both societies, but instead forged a third way, creating a new identity with a unique fur trade and Canadian history role.

Their story highlights Indigenous peoples' agency and resilience in facing colonialism. The Métis were not passive victims but active destiny shapers. They used skills and knowledge to navigate change, resist assimilation, and fight for rights as a distinct nation.

In the fur trade era context, the Métis Nation's rise is pivotal. It shows the fur trade was not just economic, but a profound cultural encounter transforming all involved. The Métis epitomize this transformation, embodying both challenges and cultural exchange opportunities on the frontier.

The Essence of the Fur Trade

What do beaver pelts, canoes, and cross-cultural alliances share? They were all essential parts of the fur trade, a phenomenon that reshaped the social, economic, and political landscape of Canada and North America. But what exactly was the fur trade, and why did it matter so much?

The fur trade was a system of economic exchange between Indigenous peoples and European traders. They exchanged animal furs and pelts, especially beaver, for European goods like guns, textiles, tools, and beads. However, this simple definition hides the complex web of relationships, power dynamics, and cultural interactions that made the fur trade transformative.

The fur trade involved several key elements:

1. Indigenous hunters and trappers harvested animal furs, primarily beaver.
2. They exchanged these furs for European goods at trading posts and through networks.
3. The furs were transported to Europe for processing into felt hats and other products.
4. Finished fur products were sold globally, driving demand for more North American pelts.
5. Transportation networks like canoe routes, portages, and posts facilitated trade.

6. Indigenous nations and European traders forged alliances and relationships.

These elements combined to create a vast, interconnected system. At its peak, it stretched from the Atlantic to the Pacific and from the Great Lakes to the Arctic. It involved dozens of Indigenous nations and European powers like the French and British.

The fur trade originated from early encounters between Indigenous peoples and European fishermen, whalers, and explorers in the 1500s. As Europeans developed a taste for beaver felt hats, they sought out Indigenous trading partners for pelts. The French established some of the first trading posts in the early 1600s, building alliances with groups like the Huron, Montagnais, and Algonquin.

Over time, the fur trade became central to the colonial economy. It shaped settlement patterns, imperial rivalries, and Indigenous-European relations. It drew Indigenous groups into new economic and political orbits, transforming traditional ways of life. New hybrid cultures emerged from the mixing of peoples.

The fur trade's impact on Canada's development can hardly be overstated. It drove European exploration and settlement, shaping the map we know today. Trading hubs like Quebec, Montreal, and Fort William became major centers. Routes like the St. Lawrence River and Great Lakes became arteries of commerce and cultural exchange.

Economically, the fur trade generated wealth for Indigenous communities and colonial powers alike. It created new markets for Indigenous goods and labor while providing a lucrative export for the French and British. Trade profits financed further expansion and development.

Socially and culturally, the fur trade was a crucible of Indigenous-European interaction. Trade alliances and intermarriage forged new relationships and hybrid identities. The trade also spread European technologies, diseases, and cultural practices into Indigenous societies, with far-reaching consequences.

Politically, the fur trade was an arena of imperial rivalry and colonial power struggles. The French and British vied for control over trading networks and Indigenous alliances, with conflicts like the Beaver Wars, a intermittent series of conflicts that started in the early 1600's and ended in 1701, and Seven Years' War that ran from 1756-1763 shifting the balance of power. For Indigenous groups, the trade offered both opportunities and risks as they navigated alliances to protect their interests.

On the ground, the fur trade involved complex protocols, rituals, and relationships. At posts and rendezvous, traders and trappers exchanged goods through rituals of gift-giving, haggling, and credit. Voyageurs and coureurs des bois ventured into Indigenous territories, learning languages and customs. Indigenous women played key roles as interpreters and guides.

The fur trade also impacted the environment, as pelt demand pressured animal populations, especially beaver. European guns and traps made hunting more efficient but destructive. Over time, depleted fur-bearers and changing European fashions led to the trade's decline in the 1800s.

Yet the fur trade's legacy endures, woven into Canadian history and identity. It shaped economic, social, and political development, leaving marks on land and peoples. It laid foundations for the modern resource economy, transport networks, and trade relationships. It also left a complex legacy of cultural interaction, dispossession, and Indigenous resilience.

In recent centuries, the fur trade has become iconic in Canadian stories, immortalized in literature, art, and popular culture. From voyageur songs to Hudson's Bay blankets, its symbols became heritage touchstones.

Ultimately, the fur trade was more than just economics or colonial history. It was a web of relationships, a cultural crucible, and a transformative force on land and peoples.

A Timeline of Transformation

To grasp the fur trade's sweeping impact on Canada's development, we must follow its journey through time. This timeline highlights the key dates, places, and figures that shaped the fur trade's evolution - from humble beginnings to its peak and eventual decline. Along the way, we'll explore the cross-cultural exchanges it enabled and its role in molding Canada's social, economic, and political fabric. By spotlighting major turning points, we'll underscore the enduring legacy of this pivotal chapter in Canadian history.

The fur trade's earliest roots stretch back to the early 1500s. European fishermen, whalers, and explorers first made contact with Indigenous peoples along the Atlantic coast during this period. These initial encounters laid the groundwork for exchanging goods like animal furs - the foundation of the future fur trade. By the late 1500s, growing European demand for beaver felt hats fueled interest in acquiring North American pelts.

In the early 1600s, the fur trade took a more structured form with the establishment of the first French trading posts:

- 1600: Pierre de Chauvin de Tonnetuit established Tadoussac, New France's first trading post, at the Saguenay and St. Lawrence Rivers' confluence.- 1603: Samuel de Champlain, considered New France's "Father," made his first voyage to Canada, paving the way for French involvement.- 1608: Champlain founded Quebec City, which became a major fur trade hub.- 1611: Henry Hudson, exploring for England, established the first English trading post at Hudson Bay, opening the door to British involvement.

As the 1600s progressed, the French forged alliances with Indigenous groups like the Huron, Montagnais, and Algonquin, who became key trading partners. The Dutch and English also gained footholds – the Dutch set up Fort Orange (present-day Albany) on the Hudson River in 1624.

The mid-1600s saw intensifying competition and conflict as rival colonial powers and Indigenous groups vied for fur trade control:

- 1634: Champlain sent Jean Nicolet to explore and trade with Great Lakes region Indigenous groups, extending French influence westward.- 1659-1667: The Beaver Wars raged heavily between the Iroquois and the Huron, Algonquin, and French allies, disrupting trade and shifting power balances.- 1670: England chartered the Hudson's Bay Company, granting it a monopoly over the fur trade in the Hudson Bay drainage basin.

Frontier Strategies: Lessons From the Fur Trade

During the fur trade era, Indigenous peoples and European traders navigated the complex economic, diplomatic, and cultural frontier landscape in clever ways. Their strategies ensured survival and facilitated trade network growth and alliances. By examining these historical tactics, we gain valuable lessons still relevant for modern business and diplomacy.

Indigenous peoples and European traders employed key strategies:

1. Adaptive trading practices
2. Alliance cultivation
3. Cultural exchange and learning
4. Economic activity diversification

5. Skilled negotiation and diplomacy

Both groups demonstrated remarkable trading practice adaptability. Indigenous communities quickly valued European goods like metal tools, firearms, and textiles, incorporating them into traditional economies. They also adapted hunting and trapping methods to meet fur demand. European traders learned to navigate Indigenous trade routes and adopted technologies like canoes and snowshoes for frontier travel.

In today's business, adapting to changing markets and consumer preferences is crucial. Companies that quickly pivot strategies and embrace new technologies or trends are more likely to succeed long-term. Similarly, understanding and adapting to cultural norms fosters productive diplomatic relationships.

Alliance building and maintenance was key to fur trade success. Indigenous communities formed alliances for access to hunting grounds, trade routes, and European goods. They allied with European traders, acting as intermediaries and guides for preferential trade terms and protection.

French traders heavily invested in Indigenous nation alliances. They participated in ceremonies like the calumet ritual which is known to many as the smoking of the peace pipe, and married into families to cement ties. These provided fur access and military support against rival European powers.

Today, companies expand market reach, access new tech, and share risks through strategic partnerships. International alliances provide cooperation frameworks for trade, security, and environmental protection.

Significant cultural exchange occurred between Indigenous peoples and Europeans. Indigenous knowledge of the land, hunting, and survival techniques were shared with traders. Europeans introduced new technologies like firearms quickly adopted by Indigenous peoples.

This exchange benefited both, enabling adaptation to frontier challenges. Europeans learned wilderness navigation, while Indigenous peoples gained tools enhancing hunting and trade capabilities.

In our globalized world, cultural exchange often remains vital for business and diplomatic success. Companies effectively navigating cultural differences and learning from diverse perspectives better succeed internationally. Diplomats investing in cultural understanding build trust and achieve objectives.

While the fur trade drove frontier economic activity, both groups diversified to mitigate risks and ensure stability. Indigenous peoples continued traditional hunting, fishing, and agriculture, providing a safety net when fur prices fluctuated. They developed new economic activities like maple sugar and wild rice production for European trade.

The Hudson's Bay Company diversified into other commodities like timber, fish, and minerals. Trading posts served as hubs for varied economic activities including agriculture and manufacturing.

Complex negotiations and diplomacy characterized the fur trade between Indigenous peoples, European traders, Indigenous nations, and European powers. Indigenous leaders skillfully negotiated, leveraging political knowledge and alliances for favorable trade terms and community protection. They played European powers against each other to maintain frontier balance.

European traders engaged in extensive diplomatic efforts to secure Indigenous trade network access. They participated in political ceremonies like gift-giving and pipe ceremonies to demonstrate respect and build trust.

Indigenous and European fur trade strategies offer valuable lessons for today. By adapting, cultivating alliances, exchanging culture and knowledge, diversifying economic activities, and excelling at negotiation and diplomacy, both thrived in a challenging, dynamic environment.

Chapter 4: Empires at War

What Sparked the Flames of Conflict?

What sparked the fierce rivalry between France and Britain in North America? This provocative question unveils ambitious desires and strategic moves that set the stage for centuries of conflict on the continent. To truly grasp the roots of this rivalry, we must explore the 18th century geopolitical landscape, where every move was calculated, and dominance over North America's vast, resource-rich territories was the ultimate prize.

Understanding the origins of this rivalry is crucial. It helps us comprehend the complex web of motivations, ambitions, and power struggles that shaped North America's history. By delving into these origins, we gain insights into the forces that drove European colonization, the impact on Indigenous peoples, and the long-lasting consequences that still influence the political, economic, and cultural landscape today.

At the core of the conflict lay a fierce competition for control over the lucrative fur trade and strategic waterways. These waterways served as arteries for commerce and transportation. Both France and Britain recognized North America's immense economic potential with its vast fur-rich forests and extensive river and lake networks facilitating trade and communication. The desire to dominate these resources and trade routes fueled an intense rivalry that would ultimately reshape the continent's map.

However, economic interests were not the sole driver. The rivalry was also deeply rooted in a centuries-old struggle for global supremacy between the two European powers. The New World became a theater where this rivalry played out, with each nation seeking to assert its dominance and expand its influence. The clash of empires on North

American soil was an extension of the political and military rivalries that had long defined the Franco-British relationship in Europe.

One misconception is that the Franco-British rivalry was a straightforward battle between two monolithic powers. In reality, the situation was far more complex, involving a web of alliances, negotiations, and power dynamics extending beyond the European players to include Indigenous nations. Both France and Britain sought to cultivate alliances with various Indigenous groups, recognizing these partnerships' crucial role in securing trade routes, gathering intelligence, and gaining military support.

The French excelled at building strong relationships with Indigenous allies through intermarriage and cultural exchange. French fur traders and missionaries, known as voyageurs and coureurs des bois, ventured deep into the continent's interior, forging close ties with Indigenous communities and learning their languages and customs. This approach allowed France to establish a vast network of alliances stretching from the Great Lakes region to the Mississippi River Valley and beyond.

In contrast, the British initially focused more on coastal settlements and were slower to penetrate the interior. However, they too recognized the importance of Indigenous alliances and sought to counter French influence by establishing their own partnerships. British colonial administrators and traders often used diplomacy, trade incentives, and military pressure to win over Indigenous allies and secure their loyalty against French competition.

The rivalry in North America was not simply two European powers vying for control over Indigenous lands. It was a complex web of interactions and power struggles involving multiple players, including Indigenous nations, colonial administrators, fur traders, and military forces. The alliances and negotiations between these various groups played a crucial role in shaping the conflict's outcome and the continent's future.

One famous example of the Franco-British rivalry was the struggle for the Ohio River Valley in the mid-18th century. This strategically important region served as a gateway to the continent's interior, becoming a flashpoint for conflict. The French sought to secure the valley by building forts and forging Indigenous alliances, while the British viewed French expansion as a threat to their colonial ambitions.

Tensions in the Ohio River Valley erupted into open warfare in 1754 when a young George Washington, then a colonial militia officer, led an attack on French forces near present-day Pittsburgh. This skirmish, the Battle of Jumonville Glen, marked the beginning of the French and Indian War, which eventually merged with the larger Seven Years' War.

The French and Indian War (1754-1763) was a turning point, pitting the French and their Indigenous allies against the British and colonial forces. The war involved military campaigns, diplomatic negotiations, and Indigenous alliances across multiple fronts, from the Ohio River Valley forests to the Quebec plains. Ultimately, the British emerged victorious, thanks to their naval power and ability to mobilize colonial resources.

The 1763 Treaty of Paris marked the end of French imperial ambitions in North America and solidified British control. France ceded its Canadian and Ohio River Valley territories to Britain, also relinquishing claims to the Louisiana Territory to Spain.

The war's consequences were far-reaching. For the British colonies, the enormously expensive war prompted new taxes and regulations to recoup costs, sparking widespread resentment and resistance among colonists who saw their rights infringed. These tensions sowed seeds for the American Revolution, exposing contradictions within the British imperial system and setting the stage for colonists to assert independence.

Today, the Franco-British rivalry's legacy lingers in North America's political, cultural, and linguistic divisions. In Canada, the conflict between French and British interests has left an imprint on the federal system and the relationship between English and French-speaking populations.

In the United States, the French and Indian War and American Revolution remain central to the national identity and mythology of throwing off British imperial rule.

Simultaneously, this legacy raises questions about colonialism, imperialism, and Indigenous displacement. The Franco-British conflict was ultimately a struggle for control over Indigenous lands and resources, consequences still reverberating today.

Battle of the Plains of Abraham: A Turning Point

On the morning of September 13, 1759, two mighty armies prepared for a pivotal battle on the Plains of Abraham near Quebec City. This clash would determine the future of North America - whether the British Empire or the French kingdom would dominate the continent. Though the battle lasted less than an hour, its outcome shaped history's course and led to the emergence of Canada as a nation.

The key figures were young British Major-General James Wolfe and his seasoned French counterpart, Louis-Joseph de Montcalm. Wolfe was renowned for boldness and tactical brilliance. The British high command tasked him with capturing Quebec, the heart of New France and key to controlling the continent. Montcalm was a veteran commander with numerous victories against the British. He fortified Quebec and vowed to defend it, knowing its fall would likely end the French empire in North America.

Wolfe faced a daunting challenge - how to attack virtually impregnable Quebec. Its natural geography atop high cliffs and the St. Lawrence River protected it. Montcalm reinforced the defenses with fortifications and a strong garrison. A frontal assault on such formidable positions would be suicidal.

Wolfe's solution was audacious. He secretly landed his troops at L'Anse-au-Foulon beach at night, using ruses like having soldiers speak French to fool sentries. In a remarkable feat, nearly 5,000 British soldiers scaled the cliffs undetected and assembled on the Plains of Abraham west of the city.

When Montcalm learned of the British on the morning of the 13th, he faced a fateful choice. His instinct was to stay within Quebec's walls, forcing the British into a disadvantageous attack or prolonged siege as winter neared. But fearing the British might entrench and cut supply lines, Montcalm decided to confront Wolfe's army in open battle.

The brief but momentous engagement followed. As the French advanced, disciplined British volleys of musket fire at close range met them. The British unleashed devastating firepower while the French struggled for a coordinated volley. Within minutes, the French attack faltered, and both Wolfe and Montcalm suffered mortal wounds.

Though a British victory, the outcome might have differed had Montcalm chosen a more cautious strategy. Remaining in Quebec's fortifications could have negated Wolfe's coup and forced an attritional battle favoring the French. Or Montcalm could have awaited reinforcements to drive Wolfe from the Plains.

Critics long debated Montcalm's rash decision and the French collapse. Some say he had little choice given being cut off, others view his actions as ill-considered. Regardless, the Battle of the Plains of Abraham proved a stunning reversal, turning stalemate into total British victory within minutes.

Quebec's fall set the stage for ending the French regime in North America and British pre-eminence's rise. Though French resistance lingered, Quebec's loss made the ultimate result inevitable. New France would become a British colony, evolving into modern Canada.

Beyond military dimensions, the battle marked a pivotal power shift enabling Britain's ascendance and setting the stage for the future

Canada. In less than an hour's musket fire outside Quebec, North America's future was determined. Nations' courses turned on individual decisions and warriors' bravery who fought and died on that fateful battlefield.

Reflecting on the Plains of Abraham over 250 years later, we see history's momentous weight and how individuals' actions profoundly impact the nations and peoples arising from the seeds planted on that blood-soaked field, though the French and British empires have long receded.

France Vs. Britain: An In-depth Comparison

In the 18th century, France and Britain, two great world powers, found themselves locked in a massive struggle for control over the vast North American continent. Although allies in other conflicts, here they were bitter rivals. Each was determined to establish their own dominance over the New World and its riches.

Despite being similar imperial powers, France and Britain approached their colonial ambitions quite differently, from military strategies to governance philosophies. These contrasts, as much as the clash of armies, ultimately determined the fate of North America.

Britain's colonial approach was rooted in commerce and settlement. They sought to establish thriving colonies populated by British subjects who would enrich the mother country through trade. This necessitated a degree of autonomy and self-governance in the colonies that centralized French control precluded. British colonists had a stake in their own defense and futures, lending a motivated manpower base for colonial militias.

France, in contrast, was more interested in resource extraction and projecting power than genuine colonization. New France was governed as a quasi-feudal system with strict hierarchies and obligations. Outside of a few core settlements, there was little drive to establish a large French population. Instead, the French focused on strategic outposts for the fur trade and military strong points. Their colonial subjects had limited self-determination, with a rigid, militarized authority structure.

These contrasting philosophies shaped how each empire pursued warfare in North America. The British leveraged their settler population advantage, raising regiments of colonial militiamen to supplement regular British army troops shipped across the Atlantic. British colonists defended their own communities, giving them a vested interest in the fight. Combined with Britain's economic might to fund, feed and equip its armies, this formed a potent force.

The French, with a much smaller settler population, relied heavily on alliances with native tribes like the Abenaki, Huron, and Wabanaki. These alliances gave crucial advantages in wilderness warfare and reconnaissance. But they also required constant diplomatic maintenance and expensive gift-giving, draining French resources. France's crack colonial regulars were formidable but few in number compared to British colonial militias.

Economically, the British colonies were powerhouses compared to New France's resource-oriented, mercantilist economy. Bustling British ports like Boston and New York, and expanding settler plantations generated vast wealth. This gave Britain financial resilience to bounce back from defeats and heavily subsidize colonial forces. New France struggled to match this, hampered by a sclerotic, quasi-feudal economic system geared towards enriching the French crown.

Initially, British forces struggled on the unfamiliar wilderness battlefield against French regiments skilled in forest warfare allied with indigenous warriors. But as the conflict continued, British generals adapted, adopting flexible light infantry tactics while leveraging manpower and logistical advantages. The huge British Royal Navy could land armies at will while cutting French supply lines, grinding down outnumbered French forces.

The French, for all their martial valor, were on borrowed time. Hemmed in by British naval power, drained by servicing native alliances, and lacking numerous motivated colonial manpower, they could slow but not halt territorial losses. With Louisbourg and Quebec's fall, supply lines from France were virtually severed. It became a mopping up action against valiant but doomed remnants like Montcalm's forces.

In the end, the contrasting imperial approaches and strengths/ weaknesses heavily shaped the outcome. France's professional but over-stretched forces geared towards projecting prestige met Britain's fully mobilized settler-soldier base and economic ability to absorb defeats. For all the French and native allies' heroism, structural disadvantages built into France's imperial model could not be overcome.

This imperial clash defined North America's future as British-dominated. The French regime's fall paved the way for the United States' emergence while sowing seeds of demographic frictions that birthed an independent Canada.

Enduringly, the tale left a poignant lesson about martial power's brittle nature without socio-economic foundations. For all France's battlefield brilliance, Britain's emerging imperial-settler colonialism, while deeply fraught, proved the stronger, more resilient template for New World power and beyond.

Seeking Peace: The Path to the Treaty of Paris

The Seven Years' War ravaged North America for years. The British and French empires relentlessly battled for supremacy over the New World's vast territories. Their alliances with Indigenous nations added complexity to the colonial rivalries. As the battles raged, it became clear that the path forward required not just military might but also skillful diplomacy and compromise.

The war took an immense toll. Lives were lost, resources depleted, and once-promising colonies lay in ruins. Though victorious, the British faced mounting debts and discontent among colonists. The defeated French grappled with losing their prized North American possessions. Indigenous nations found themselves caught between rival powers, their lands and lifestyles threatened. A resolution was needed to prevent plunging the continent back into chaos.

Continued conflict risked dire consequences. Without stability, colonies would struggle to rebuild and prosper. Disrupted trade would hinder economic growth, leaving populations in hardship. Strains on imperial finances risked inciting unrest and rebellion. Moreover, unchecked animosity between the British, French, and Indigenous peoples threatened generational cycles of violence – a grim future all sides sought to avoid.

Yet the path to peace was challenging. Bitter rivalries, conflicting claims, and deep mistrust made negotiations delicate. As victors, the British sought dominance over North America. Though weakened, the French aimed to retain a New World foothold and protect colonies. Indigenous nations fought to safeguard sovereignty and ancestral lands. Finding common ground amid diverging interests would test diplomacy's limits.

Still, visionary statesmen recognized peace as the only viable path. They saw an opportunity to forge a new equilibrium based on negotiation, concession, and coexistence. A bold vision, but one offering hope for stability and prosperity.

The 1763 Treaty of Paris culminated this arduous journey. Through diplomacy and hard-fought compromises, the warring parties bridged differences and reshaped North America's map. The dominant British took control of vast territories, including coveted New France lands. The diminished French retained Caribbean islands and Newfoundland fishing rights. Indigenous nations, though not formally recognized, remained vital presences with influential alliances and territorial claims.

The treaty did not erase war's scars but provided a foundation for a new order. Establishing clear boundaries reduced future conflict risks and created colonial growth potential. The British envisioned their new territories as a vast North American empire rivaling Europe's.

However, the treaty's true significance lay in the precedent for peaceful coexistence. It proved even bitter rivals could find common ground through dialogue and compromise – difficult but preferable to endless war. Most importantly, it paved the way for North America's peoples – British, French, Indigenous, and eventually Canadian – to thrive together through shared commitment to peace and prosperity.

The path from the Treaty of Paris to Canada's birth was not straight, bringing new challenges, conflicts, and growth opportunities. But the treaty laid the groundwork, showing a better future was possible if all sides worked for it.

A Chronology of Conflict

To understand the clash between France and Britain for control of North America, we need to examine the timeline of conflicts that shaped the continent's destiny. By exploring this chronology of violence, from early skirmishes to the decisive Battle of the Plains of Abraham and its diplomatic aftermath, we gain valuable insights into the forces that forged Canada.

The roots of French and British rivalry trace back to the early 1500s. In 1534, French explorer Jacques Cartier claimed land along the St. Lawrence River for France, establishing a foothold. The British followed in 1607 by founding Jamestown, Virginia. As both empires expanded, conflict was inevitable.

Key events include:

1. King William's War (1688-1697): French and British colonists, along with indigenous allies, raided each other's settlements. The Treaty of Ryswick ended fighting but tensions remained high.

2. Queen Anne's War (1702-1713): The British captured France's Port Royal stronghold in Acadia (present-day Nova Scotia). The Treaty

of Utrecht forced France to cede Hudson Bay, Newfoundland, and Acadia.

3. King George's War (1744-1748): The French scored a stunning victory at Louisbourg. The Treaty of Aix-la-Chapelle returned Louisbourg to France in exchange for Madras, India.

4. The French and Indian War leading into The Seven Years' War (1754-1763): This climactic struggle for supremacy began in the Ohio Valley and spread globally. Key turning points:

- The Battle of Fort Necessity (1754): A young George Washington surrendered to French forces.

- The Battle of the Monongahela (1755): British General Edward Braddock's forces were routed.

- The Fall of Fort Oswego (1756) and Fort William Henry (1757): Major British losses.

- The Siege of Louisbourg (1758): The British captured this French fortress.

- The Battle of Fort Carillon (1758): The French under Montcalm repelled a British assault.

- The Battle of Quebec (1759): Wolfe's forces scaled cliffs to the Plains of Abraham, defeating and fatally wounding Montcalm.

- The Battle of Sainte-Foy (1760): A French victory, but the British held firm.

- The Surrender of Montreal (1760): The French capitulated, marking New France's fall.

The Treaty of Paris (1763) ended the war. France ceded Canada and most North American possessions to Britain. However, Britain's relationship with its colonies had changed. Without French threats, many colonists resented British rule, sparking the American Revolution (1775-1783).

Though Britain lost its Thirteen Colonies, it kept Canada. Here, generations of conflict and cooperation intertwined French and British identities. The Quebec Act of 1774 guaranteed religious freedom for

Catholics and restored French civil law, laying the groundwork for a dual English-French Canadian identity.

Loyalists fleeing the American Revolution settled in Canada, bringing a new British identity. Yet the quest for French-British coexistence continued, seen in milestones like the Constitutional Act of 1791 dividing Quebec, the Act of Union in 1840 reuniting it as the Province of Canada, and ultimately Confederation in 1867 birthing the new nation.

The 1982 patriation of the Constitution with its Charter of Rights and Freedoms reflected this ongoing balance. Today, Canada stands as a testament to its history - forged in French-British rivalry, shaped by the struggle for supremacy, and now defined by weaving diverse strands into a unique identity.

The Human Cost: An Evidence-Based Analysis

To truly understand the immense struggle between France and Britain for control of North America, we must look beyond battle dates and treaties. We need to see the human cost of this relentless conflict - the toll paid by soldiers, civilians, and indigenous peoples in the name of imperial ambition.

The most direct impact was the horrific loss of life on battlefields. In 1759 at the Battle of Quebec, British forces under General Wolfe lost around 655 killed or wounded, while the French under Montcalm suffered approximately 840 casualties, including both commanders dying. The next year at the Battle of Sainte-Foy, the French lost about 840 men and the British 1,102.

But major battles were just a fraction of the lives lost. Skirmishes, raids, sieges, disease, and exposure steadily claimed more victims. Exact numbers are uncertain, but estimates suggest France lost around 16,000-20,000 soldiers in North America during the Seven Years' War alone, while British losses numbered 10,000-15,000 - not counting thousands of indigenous warriors who died fighting alongside the Europeans.

The devastation reached far beyond the front lines. Civilians endured violence, displacement, starvation, and disease disrupting their lives. The brutal Acadian Expulsion of 1755-1764 saw the British forcibly remove about 11,500 French settlers from Nova Scotia and New Brunswick. Many Acadians perished from shipwrecks, illness in crowded camps, or exposure when left to fend for themselves. Survivors faced trauma and struggle to rebuild.

Indigenous peoples suffered upheaval as they were caught between rival empires. Traditional ways of life were shattered. Exposure to European diseases like smallpox decimated populations with no immunity. In 1763, British agent William Trent described villages that once had 100-300 people reduced to just 15-20 survivors, many dying.

The scars weren't just physical. Soldiers, settlers, and indigenous peoples grappled with what we now call PTSD. Private Andrew McDougal of the British 78th Regiment wrote home after Quebec, haunted by "the groans, cries, and...howlings of the Indians, scarcely bearable to the ear." Though trauma wasn't openly discussed then, the impact surely echoed across generations.

Yet amid such misery were glimmers of humanity. French and British soldiers sometimes showed mercy to enemies. One account tells of British troops finding a gravely wounded French soldier at Sainte-Foy, left for dead. Instead of abandoning him, they carried him to their hospital and tended his wounds until he could return home. Rare moments like these remind us of our capacity for empathy, even in darkness.

Civilians showed astounding resilience too. Separated Acadian families fought to reunite and preserve their identity, some returning home years later. Indigenous peoples drew strength from traditions and kinship to weather war's storms. Their fortitude in unimaginable challenges is a testament to our ability to endure.

Facing this human toll of war, it's tempting to give in to despair or cynicism. But there are also glimmers of hope - in a soldier's compassion, a civilian's perseverance, a survivor's resilience. The greatest lesson may be recognizing our shared humanity across conflict's divides.

The French and British struggle for North America reshaped history. Yet it was also a profoundly human story - thousands of lives caught in the currents of nations battling.

Chapter 5: Birth of a Nation

Daring Dreams: Who Imagined a United Canada?

What daring dreamers first imagined a united Canada, a patchwork of provinces spanning a vast continent? The brilliant and passionate minds of the Fathers of Confederation conceived this bold vision, fraught with challenges. Who were these intrepid nation-builders? They deftly navigated conflicting interests and forged an improbable alliance, laying the foundation for a new country's birth.

To grasp Confederation's monumental achievement, we must understand its principal architects' hearts and minds. Exploring who dreamed of a united Canada goes beyond historical footnotes; it delves into our national identity's fabric. The drive for Confederation exceeded political expediency or economic necessity; it was a grand vision of a nation stretching from sea to sea, a mosaic of diverse peoples united.

The road to Confederation was treacherous, beset by regional rivalries, cultural differences, and divergent economic interests. The Fathers faced formidable challenges: reconciling French Canada's aspirations with English Canada's ambitions, bridging the vast geographical divide, and persuading autonomous colonies to cede power to a central government.

While many historians portray Confederation as inevitable due to geopolitical realities, this overlooks the endeavor's sheer audacity and proponents' indomitable will. Confederation wasn't a foregone conclusion; it was a daring gambit, a leap into an uncertain future.

Practical considerations like needing common defense, economic integration, and a transcontinental railway played a role. But the conventional narrative doesn't capture the driving idealism and force of personality. To truly understand Confederation's origins, we must look beyond history books into the Fathers' hearts and minds.

Sir John A. Macdonald was more than a pragmatist. He was a visionary who glimpsed greatness in a united Canada, not just a larger political entity but a distinctly Canadian identity forged through Confederation. For Macdonald, Confederation created a strong, centralized government to withstand regionalism and resist outside influence. His vision: a Canada succeeding the British Empire, taking its place among world powers.

George-Étienne Cartier protected Quebec's interests but was also a nation-builder. He saw Confederation securing French Canada's survival within a larger framework, recognizing the Canadian experience's duality.

Thomas D'Arcy McGee envisioned Canada exemplifying diversity and tolerance, a harmonious, pluralistic society. His 1868 assassination deprived Canada of an idealistic voice, but his vision endures.

The Fathers weren't perfect, but extraordinary men with vision and courage. They set aside differences to work toward a shared cause, dreaming of a nation not yet existing, one greater than its parts. They dared make that dream reality.

On Confederation's 150th anniversary, it's tempting to take Canada for granted, assuming inevitability. But Canada wasn't inevitable; it resulted from human agency, individuals dreaming big with courage and determination to make it real.

Crafting Unity: Confederation Explained

To truly appreciate the incredible achievement of Confederation, we need to understand two key concepts: "Confederation" itself and "Identity." Although simple on the surface, these terms capture the complicated political, social, and cultural forces that shaped Canada's birth as a nation.

"Confederation" is often used interchangeably with "union," but it has a distinct, nuanced meaning. A union implies a complete merger into one homogeneous whole. Confederation, however, suggests a more delicate balance - a coming together of diverse elements that retain their unique traits while forming a cohesive entity. This distinction is crucial to understanding the genius behind Canadian Confederation.

The Fathers didn't seek to erase differences between colonies. They recognized the diversity as a strength, not a weakness. They envisioned a nation where constituent parts could maintain cultural, linguistic, and historical identities while cooperating within a larger framework.

The Canadian identity emerging from Confederation wasn't rigid or prescriptive. It was flexible and inclusive, allowing multiple loyalties - one could be French and Canadian, English and Canadian, or Indigenous and Canadian simultaneously. This pluralistic understanding of identity radically departed from prevailing 19th century ideas of nationhood.

Forging this shared identity wasn't easy. It required navigating deep tensions, especially between French and English Canada. The Fathers had to reassure French Canadians that their language, culture and religious rights would be protected within a largely English-speaking country. Simultaneously, they convinced English Canadians that accommodating French Canadian distinctiveness wouldn't undermine national unity.

Their ingenious solution: a federal system dividing powers between the central and provincial governments. This allowed regional autonomy and cultural preservation alongside a strong national government transcending local differences. It was a delicate balancing act requiring great political skill and willingness to compromise.

But beyond politics, it was a leap of faith - believing diverse backgrounds, languages and religions could unite to build a shared future. It demanded trusting diversity could fuel strength and resilience rather than division and weakness.

Of course, the Canadian identity evolved since 1867, embracing new immigrants, cultures, languages and understandings of Indigenous rights.

Ultimately, Confederation's story is one of possibility - building a nation not on ethnic homogeneity but shared values and aspirations. It reminds us diversity isn't a challenge but a strength to embrace.

The Charlottetown Conference: A Turning Point

In September 1864, a pivotal gathering occurred in Charlottetown, Prince Edward Island that forever altered the course of Canadian history. Delegates from the British North American colonies of Nova Scotia, New Brunswick, Prince Edward Island, and the Province of Canada (present-day Ontario and Quebec) came together. This case study explores the crucial discussions, debates, and decisions made during this conference that laid the foundation for a united Canada.

Some of the era's most influential political figures attended the Charlottetown Conference. John A. Macdonald and George-Étienne Cartier represented the Province of Canada. Charles Tupper came from Nova Scotia, Samuel Leonard Tilley from New Brunswick, and George Coles from Prince Edward Island. Despite diverse backgrounds and regional interests, these men shared a vision of a stronger, more prosperous future for British North America.

The growing threat of American expansionism and need for greater economic cooperation among colonies brought these leaders together. After the American Civil War ended, fears arose that the victorious North might turn northward. Additionally, the colonies faced economic pressures, including improving trade relations and infrastructure development. The Charlottetown Conference presented an opportunity to address these challenges through forming a united federation.

Delegates engaged in intense, wide-ranging discussions. They debated the merits of a federal versus legislative union, the division of powers between central and provincial governments, and the representation of each province in the proposed federal parliament. Macdonald and Cartier strongly argued for a centralized federal system, while Maritime delegates, especially from Prince Edward Island, favored a more decentralized structure protecting their autonomy.

Through skillful negotiation and compromise, the delegates reached consensus on general principles. They agreed on a federal system with a strong central government while preserving provincial identities and powers. The conference also laid groundwork for protecting minority rights, particularly French Canadians', through provisions for using English and French in the federal parliament and courts.

Delegates left the Charlottetown Conference with a shared sense of purpose and commitment to creating a united Canada, paving the way for the Quebec Conference later that year to further refine the Confederation plan. In 1867, the British Parliament passed the British North America Act, officially establishing the Dominion of Canada.

The Charlottetown Conference succeeded due to several factors. First, delegates approached discussions with a spirit of compromise and willingness to set aside regional differences for the greater good. Second, skilled negotiators like Macdonald and Cartier provided leadership, bridging divides and finding common ground. Finally, delegates were driven by a shared urgency, recognizing the time for action had arrived.

Critics argue the Conference was dominated by political elite interests and inadequately addressed marginalized groups' concerns, particularly Indigenous peoples. While focused primarily on British North American colonies and European settlers' interests, we must recognize the Conference as a product of its time and appreciate the significant progress it represented in political cooperation and nation-building.

The Charlottetown Conference marked a turning point in Canadian history, setting the stage for creating a united Canada. The vision, leadership, and compromise demonstrated by delegates continue inspiring Canadians as we work towards building a more inclusive, prosperous, and sustainable nation.

Colonies in Contrast: Before Confederation

In the early days of British North America, the colonies that would eventually form Canada had stark contrasts. They were connected to the British Empire and desired prosperity, but each had its own distinct character shaped by geography, economy, and settlers' origins. It was like siblings raised in one household yet developing unique personalities and aspirations.

The future Canadian colonies stretched across a vast expanse from the Atlantic to the Pacific. In the east were the Maritime colonies of Nova Scotia, New Brunswick, and Prince Edward Island. Their economies heavily depended on the sea through fishing, shipbuilding, and trade. They had a long history of self-government and strong regional identities.

In contrast, the Province of Canada (later Ontario and Quebec) was landlocked with a more diversified economy. It had a larger population and complex political landscape, with tensions between English and French-speaking populations. The Province had a more developed bicameral legislature and responsible government.

To the west lay British Columbia nerds Vancouver Island, isolated from the rest by the Rocky Mountains. These sparsely populated colonies had economies based on resource extraction like gold mining and forestry. They had a frontier character and were less politically developed than eastern colonies.

Economic structures differed greatly between colonies. The Maritimes depended heavily on trade with the United States and a mercantile economy. They relied more on subsistence agriculture with less manufacturing. The Province of Canada had a diversified economy with growing manufacturing, canals, and railways.

Social and cultural makeups also varied significantly. The Maritimes had more homogenous British-descent populations. The Province of Canada had a sizable French-speaking population, especially in Lower Canada (Quebec). This linguistic and cultural divide would challenge the journey to Confederation.

Political systems across colonies also differed widely. The Maritimes had elected assemblies and autonomy from Britain but with powerful appointed legislative councils that could block legislation. The Province of Canada had an elected assembly and appointed council, with tensions over English-French representation and language rights.

Despite differences, the colonies shared being part of the British Empire with allegiance to the Crown. They had similar British common law legal systems, though Quebec followed the French civil code. They desired economic growth, trade, infrastructure like transportation, and saw benefits in cooperation.

However, the path to Confederation faced obstacles like regional rivalries, economic disparities, and cultural differences. Concerns existed over loss of autonomy and domination by larger colonies. Representation in a united government was a key issue, with the Maritimes fearing being overshadowed by Ontario and Quebec's populations.

The 1864 Charlottetown Conference proved pivotal by bringing colonial delegates together to discuss union. Despite differences, they found common ground and laid Confederation's foundation. The Quebec Conference later refined the union plan.

In 1867, the British North America Act created the Canadian federation with a strong central government and powerful provinces. It protected minority rights, particularly for French Canadians.

Today, Canada remains vibrant and diverse with a strong national identity. However, regional and cultural divisions persist with tensions over issues like equalization payments and federal-provincial powers.

Pre-Confederation was complex with vast geographic, economic, social, and political contrasts between colonies. Yet they overcame challenges to unite, leaving a legacy Canada still grapples with regarding regional identities and cultural diversity. Understanding this period appreciation the remarkable Confederation achievement and ongoing nation-building efforts.

Uniting a Nation: Overcoming the Obstacles

Leading up to Confederation, the path toward a united Canada faced massive challenges that nearly derailed the entire endeavor. Regional disputes, economic imbalances, and cultural differences cast a dark shadow over the dream of a unified nation. Yet, Canada's founding fathers overcame these daunting obstacles through remarkable ingenuity and innovative solutions that paved the way for birthing a new country.

One pressing issue they confronted was deep-rooted regional rivalries dividing the colonies. Each region had its distinct identity shaped by history, geography, and economic interests. The Maritime provinces feared their fisheries and shipbuilding industries would be overshadowed by the more populous Canada West and Canada East. Meanwhile, the western frontier worried a distant central government would neglect their untamed wilderness.

If unresolved, these tensions risked tearing apart the fragile unity before it even formed. Failure meant a fractured set of weakened colonies vulnerable to U.S. expansionist ambitions and unable to reach their full potential. The stakes could not be higher.

The founding fathers knew they needed to bridge the divides separating the colonies. They understood the key was crafting a political system accommodating each region's diverse interests and aspirations while providing a strong, stable central government.

Their ingenious solution: a federal system dividing power between a central authority and regional governments. The federal government would manage national matters like defense, foreign affairs, and the economy. Provinces would control local issues like education, healthcare, and natural resources.

To implement this, the founders engaged in intense negotiations, traveling across colonies and meeting local leaders to build Confederation support. They worked tirelessly finding common ground and compromises satisfying each region's competing demands.

A breakthrough came at the 1864 Quebec Conference where delegates from Canada, Nova Scotia, and New Brunswick shaped the proposed federation's details. Over three heated weeks, they gradually formed the blueprint for the new nation that became the British North America Act establishing the Dominion of Canada in 1867.

While some advocated for a centralized state or looser confederation, the federal system proved most viable, striking a balance between national unity and regional autonomy. It allowed a strong central government providing leadership while respecting each province's unique identity and interests.

The federal system's success is seen in Canada's 150 years of stability and prosperity. Despite challenges like economic recessions and constitutional disputes, it remained resilient and adaptable. Canada exemplifies what visionary leaders can achieve through creativity, determination, and the spirit of compromise in confronting daunting problems.

A Timeline of Unity

Canada's path to Confederation was long and winding, shaped by visionary leaders, heated debates, and pivotal events that would determine the nation's destiny. The desire for unity sprouted long before 1867 as the British North American colonies grappled with challenges around growth, security, and self-governance.

The timeline kicked off in the early 1800s, a period of change and uncertainty across the colonies. In 1841, the Act of Union merged Upper and Lower Canada into one province. This aimed to ease tensions between English and French-speaking colonists, though it also planted seeds for future conflicts over representation and power-sharing.

As the colonies expanded and prospered, their craving for autonomy and self-determination grew stronger. A pivotal 1864 conference in Charlottetown brought together Maritime delegates to discuss a potential union. This expanded to include Canada, shifting conversations toward a grander vision of a united British North America.

Charlottetown paved the way for the Quebec Conference later that year, where the 72 Resolutions were drafted. These formed the basis of the British North America Act, outlining divisions of federal and provincial powers, the parliamentary system's structure, and protection of minority rights.

Yet, the road to Confederation had obstacles. Debates raged in the Province of Canada over a federal versus legislative union's merits. Concerns swirled around losing autonomy and protecting French Canadian rights. In the Maritimes, fears brewed over being overshadowed by larger provinces and losing local control.

Despite challenges, the Fathers of Confederation persevered, driven by a vision of a strong, united nation that could defend itself and prosper amidst a changing world. Leaders like John A. Macdonald,

George-Étienne Cartier, and George Brown tirelessly built consensus and rallied support.

In 1866, the London Conference finalized the British North America Act's details, later passed by British Parliament with Queen Victoria's royal assent. On July 1, 1867, the Dominion of Canada was born, uniting Ontario, Quebec, Nova Scotia, and New Brunswick under a federal government.

Citizens across the new nation celebrated their shared identity and purpose amid the joyous fanfare. But Confederation marked just the beginning. In years and decades ahead, Canada would face new challenges and opportunities in building a just, prosperous, and inclusive society.

The addition of new provinces and territories expanded Canada's borders and diversity. Manitoba, Northwest Territories, British Columbia, and Prince Edward Island joined between 1870-1873. The Yukon Territory and parts of the Northwest Territories followed in 1898, then Alberta and Saskatchewan in 1905.

As Canada grew, so did its national identity. It weathered external threats and internal struggles, from the Riel Rebellions to conscription crises of the World Wars. Yet Canadians remained united by shared democratic values, freedom, and rule of law.

Chapter 6: Railways and Rebellion

Who Dared to Dream of Iron Paths?

Can you imagine Canada without railroads? Without those vast iron paths connecting the patchwork of provinces from coast to coast? Canada as we know it today might not exist without the grand ambition of the Canadian Pacific Railway (CPR).

This audacious dream was about much more than just laying tracks - it was about nation-building. After Confederation, Canada struggled to establish its identity and assert sovereignty as a young country. Building the CPR united the far-flung provinces, secured the western frontier against American expansion, and opened vast lands for settlement and economic development.

But who were the visionaries behind this colossal undertaking? Who had the foresight, determination, and sheer audacity to propose such a project before heavy machinery and modern engineering existed?

The CPR's story features larger-than-life personalities, political intrigue, and unwavering resolve against daunting obstacles. It's a tale of men who dared to dream big and risked everything to make their vision a reality.

At the forefront stood Sir John A. Macdonald, Canada's first Prime Minister. Macdonald saw the railway as integral to his vision of a united Canada spanning from sea to sea. He famously declared, "We must have a great highway from the Atlantic to the Pacific, entirely on Canadian soil." Despite opposition and setbacks, Macdonald never wavered.

Alongside Macdonald were George Stephen and Donald Smith, the CPR's principal financiers. These self-made Scottish-Canadian businessmen staked their fortunes and reputations on the railway. They assembled investors and lobbied tirelessly for government support, despite skepticism.

Engineers and surveyors plotted the route through challenging terrain like the muskeg swamps of northern Ontario and the Rocky Mountains. Men like Sandford Fleming, the Chief Engineer, and Major Albert Bowman Rogers, who discovered the Selkirk Mountains pass bearing his name.

Thousands of laborers, many Chinese immigrants, toiled in brutal conditions laying tracks. They blasted tunnels, bridged chasms, and inched across treacherous mountain passes. Many lost their lives.

Against all odds, these men persevered through scandals, disputes, and cost overruns. The last spike in 1885 marked the completion of a railway transforming Canada forever.

While history focuses on the great men, the CPR resulted from a collective effort, vision, and willingness to take risks for the greater good.

The common perception then was that a transcontinental railway was foolish - too vast, expensive, and risky. Many argued Canada lacked the population and economic clout. London financial markets saw it as speculative with little prospect of return.

But the visionaries saw beyond immediate challenges to a future where the railway opened new markets, spurred immigration and settlement, and bound the nation with steel bands.

Their approach drew controversy. The CPR syndicate demanded substantial subsidies and land grants, which critics called corporate welfare. Questions arose about the route, standards, and treatment of workers, especially discriminated Chinese laborers facing danger.

Yet Macdonald, Stephen, Smith and others' vision proved right. The CPR became the nation's transportation backbone, economic growth engine, and symbol of unity. It's success offers lessons for today's visionaries. It shows the importance of thinking big, looking beyond obstacles to long-term potential. It demonstrates public-private partnership's power, with government and business united. It reminds us great achievements often require sacrifice and risk.

Of course, the CPR's legacy has darker chapters too - Indigenous displacement, exploited immigrant labor, environmental impact. But looking forward, we can draw inspiration from those who dared dream big for a higher purpose.

The Great Gamble: Financing the Dream

In Canadian history, few endeavors fire the imagination like the construction of the Canadian Pacific Railway. This massive project promised to unite a vast nation, open up untapped lands and resources, and pave the way for prosperity. However, the path to realizing this grand vision was treacherous, filled with financial perils. Our study takes us back to the 1880s when the CPR teetered on the brink of ruin. Only the audacity and skill of a handful of bold financiers kept the dream of a transcontinental railway alive.

The central players were businessmen led by George Stephen and Donald Smith. These risk-takers had already amassed fortunes in banking, railroads, and other ventures. But the CPR represented a challenge on an entirely different scale. Daunting geographical obstacles, sparse population, and economic uncertainty made many dismiss it as a foolhardy gamble doomed to fail.

The crux was money. Building a railway across the vast Canadian expanse required staggering sums of capital. Government support fell far short. Stephen, Smith, and colleagues had to swiftly raise the bulk of funds themselves before momentum fizzled.

Their strategy showcased financial ingenuity. First, they tapped their extensive networks, convincing wealthy individuals and institutions to buy into the CPR's potential riches in the Canadian west. Next, they issued company bonds and shares on the financial markets - a risky move with not a single mile of track laid. But Stephen and Smith held an ace - they used the government's land grants as collateral for loans, arguing the land would become immensely valuable. It was a persuasive pitch that unlocked the floodgates of money.

Yet with influxes of capital, the CPR constantly strained under soaring construction costs that often outpaced funds. Collapse seemed inevitable at times. But Stephen, Smith, and allies persevered relentlessly. They poured personal wealth into the project, rallied new investors, and lobbied government for support. It was an all-consuming effort.

It paid off spectacularly in 1885 when, despite setbacks, the final spike was driven at Craigellachie, B.C. The impossible dream was realized - a railway spanning the continent from Atlantic to Pacific united Canada and expanded its economic horizons immeasurably.

While CPR's builders get credit for their vision and determination, the financial prowess of men like Stephen and Smith proved equally pivotal. Without their ability to mobilize capital, navigate markets, and mitigate risks, the railway would have remained a pipe dream. Their gamble paid off big time.

Critics argue the financiers' methods exploited others to line their own pockets. Questions linger about government concessions made to the CPR and impacts on Indigenous peoples and the environment. Valid scrutiny is needed.

Yet one fact is sure - financing the CPR marked a watershed moment in Canadian history. It showcased the power of private capital to drive national development for good or ill. It highlighted the young nation's business elite's ingenuity and resourcefulness which left an indelible economic imprint.

Reflecting on this case rouses awe over the scale of challenges predecessors confronted and the boldness of their solutions. The CPR embodied what vision, determination, and financial daring could achieve. It imparts a lasting lesson as we tackle modern infrastructure and economic frontiers - to draw inspiration from this saga and never shy from audacious gambles in pursuit of grand national visions.

Steel Vs. Spirit: The Indigenous Resistance

The Canadian Pacific Railway stretched across our vast nation, a vision of unity and progress. But for Indigenous peoples, these steel tracks symbolized division and displacement that threatened ancient ways of life. The conflicting worldviews – industrialization's relentless march versus a deep-rooted connection to the land – defined a pivotal chapter in Canada's history.

We must contrast the motivations driving the CPR builders and Indigenous communities. For the railway company, the goal united distant Canadian regions, opened new markets and opportunities, and asserted the young nation's place globally. The land was a resource to tame, a frontier to conquer for progress and prosperity. But Indigenous peoples cherished and protected the sacred land, the source of their physical, spiritual, and cultural sustenance. Dividing and scarring the earth with spikes and tracks opposed deeply-held beliefs and traditions.

As the railway pushed westward, these worldviews collided intensely. Indigenous communities saw hunting grounds bisected, sacred sites desecrated by crews, and lifestyles disrupted by settlers and speculators. Many were forcibly relocated, homes and villages destroyed, families separated. But Indigenous peoples bravely resisted to protect lands, cultures, and ways of life. Some attacked railway crews and sabotaged tracks and equipment. Others sought treaties and agreements guaranteeing rights and autonomy.

Even while resisting, Indigenous peoples adapted and survived adversity. Some found work as laborers, guides, and interpreters. Others used the railway to travel and forge new alliances. Their resilience and refusal to be erased or assimilated testifies to an indomitable spirit. The railway's legacy includes both unity and division, triumph and tragedy, hope and heartbreak.

A Nation Divided: The Métis Uprising

In the late 1800s, the western prairies of Canada witnessed a historic struggle. The Métis people, with Indigenous and European roots, fought for their land, rights, and way of life. As Canada expanded westward, the Métis, led by Louis Riel, stood against the rising colonial forces.

The conflict had deep cultural, political, and economic roots. For the Métis, the vast prairies were integral to their identity—the land was their sacred lifeblood passed down through generations. But as settlers arrived and the government disregarded Métis land rights, tensions boiled over. The influx threatened their hunting grounds, river lot settlements, and very existence as a people.

Inaction meant catastrophe. The Métis faced being marginalized, their culture eroded, livelihoods destroyed. Losing their land would sever their spiritual tie to the earth. And the government's refusal to acknowledge their land claims and status endangered their existence.

Louis Riel emerged as a beacon of hope and resistance. The passionate leader understood the Métis' survival hinged on asserting their rights and defending their homeland. He rallied them, forging Indigenous alliances and transforming the Métis into a formidable force. Under Riel, they established a provisional government, drafted rights, and demanded recognition.

But resolution proved challenging. Prime Minister John A. Macdonald viewed the resistance as a threat to national unity and western expansion. He deployed troops, sparking violent clashes at Duck Lake, Fish Creek, and Batoche. Though brave and ingenious, the outnumbered Métis fell to superior Canadian forces.

Riel's capture, trial, and execution crushed the resistance. But the uprising exposed deep inequalities and brought Indigenous peoples' plight into focus. Gradually, the government addressed Métis land claims and Indigenous political and cultural rights.

While defeated militarily, the Métis resistance resonated powerfully. Louis Riel became a rallying cry for Indigenous activists seeking self-determination and equality. The struggle embodied the resilience of a people refusing to be silenced or erased.

Looking back, we see the Métis uprising laid bare Canada's colonial faultlines and the challenge of building an inclusive society.

The Iron Ribbon: Symbol of Unity or Division?

In 1885, a cheer echoed across Canada as the last spike was driven into the Canadian Pacific Railway. This steel ribbon stretching from the Atlantic to the Pacific was praised as a symbol of unity - a tangible dream of a united Canada come true. But was it truly a unifying force? Or did it highlight and worsen the deep divisions within the young nation?

At its core, the Canadian Pacific Railway was an extraordinary engineering and human achievement. It connected distant provinces, enabling the flow of goods, people, and ideas across a vast, often harsh landscape. In this sense, it undeniably bridged the disparate parts of Canada into one whole. The railway allowed an Ontario farmer to sell wheat to a baker in British Columbia. It let families in Quebec start new lives on the Prairies. It created a shared economy and identity - a sense that all Canadians belonged to something greater, no matter their location or background.

However, the railway's construction and operation also exposed profound societal divisions. Most glaring was the treatment of Indigenous peoples whose ancestral lands it crossed. Building the railway required acquiring vast lands, often through treaties misunderstood by Indigenous signatories and dishonored by the government. It disrupted traditional ways of life, cut through sacred sites, and enabled a wave of settlement that fundamentally shifted the West's population and power balance. For many Indigenous communities, the railway symbolized not unity, but dispossession and erosion of their culture and autonomy.

The railway also highlighted ethnic and class divides within Canada. The diverse construction workforce reflected the inequality of the time. European immigrants, largely British and Eastern European, filled many skilled roles. Meanwhile, recruited Chinese laborers endured dangerous, grueling work laying track through the Rockies while denied equal rights and protections as their white counterparts. Even after completion, the railway reinforced class distinctions with its luxurious Pullman cars catering to the wealthy while poorer passengers crowded into basic coaches.

Furthermore, the CPR became politically divisive, fueling regional resentment. Routing the main line through the southern Prairies, while economically logical, felt like betrayal to many in the North and East - a concession to American interests. The railway's monopoly and government ties also bred suspicion, especially among farmers feeling gouged on shipping rates for their goods.

Yet the CPR undeniably helped forge a Canadian identity. It made the idea of a transcontinental Canada feel tangible - a country spanning vast landscapes and peoples. Its construction story, with tales of heroism and hardship, became part of the nation's folklore, a testament to Canadian grit. And by enabling western settlement, the railway helped shape a distinct Canadian society as immigrants adapted together to frontier challenges, creating communities neither British nor American, but uniquely Canadian.

In the end, the CPR embodied both the promise and contradictions of the Canadian project. It brought Canadians together while highlighting their divisions. It symbolized that unity is a constant work-in-progress requiring continuous negotiation, not a given.

Timelines Collide: The Railway Through History

To truly understand the significance of the Canadian Pacific Railway, we want to explore its remarkable journey through history. This timeline chronicles the key milestones, challenges, and relentless progress that forged Canada's identity on the transcontinental railroad tracks.

The idea of a transcontinental railway took root in the early 19th century. In 1829, British-Canadian explorer Sir George Simpson first proposed linking the Atlantic and Pacific oceans by rail. Although met with skepticism initially, this seed would eventually bloom into a defining Canadian landmark.

As the 19th century progressed, the need for a coast-to-coast railway grew increasingly apparent. The scattered British North American colonies required reliable transportation and communication to unite them. In 1867, the year of Canada's Confederation, the new constitution enshrined a promise to begin railway construction within two years.

However, political disputes and economic hurdles delayed the project's start until 1875. That year, Prime Minister Alexander Mackenzie's government broke ground near Fort William, Ontario (now Thunder Bay), marking the arduous journey's beginning.

Constructing the railway was an immense feat of engineering and human endurance. The route traversed challenging terrains - from the rugged Canadian Shield to the towering Rockies. Thousands of workers, including many European and Asian immigrants, toiled in harsh conditions to lay the nation-binding tracks.

Progress was often slow and costly. Early years saw financial troubles and the Pacific Scandal of 1873, nearly derailing the entire enterprise. Yet construction persevered. In 1880, the government contracted the Canadian Pacific Railway Company to complete the project.

Under William Van Horne's dynamic leadership, construction accelerated dramatically. His legendary drive pushed crews to lay up to six miles of track daily, racing westward.

As it snaked across the land, the railway left an indelible mark. It opened the Prairies for settlement by European and American immigrants. It facilitated new industries like agriculture and mining, fueling the western economy. But it also disrupted Indigenous peoples' traditional territories and livelihoods.

The Chinese laborers' crucial yet overlooked contributions cannot be forgotten. Thousands endured backbreaking labor, discrimination, and dangers to tackle the most challenging sections. Many lost their lives in pursuit of the railway dream.

In November 1885, after years of toil, the final spike - a golden one - was driven at Craigellachie, BC. The Canadian Pacific Railway spanned the continent, a triumph of resilience and determination.

The railway's completion sparked national pride and unity. It symbolized adversity overcome, binding distant provinces as one. In following years, it facilitated western settlement, resource development, and the growth of towns on its route.

Beyond economics, the railway fostered cultural exchange and identity. It connected diverse Canadians, facilitating ideas' spread across vast distances like never before.

The 20th century saw the railway diversify into steamships, hotels, and telecom while aiding the World War I war effort. Though challenged by automobiles and airlines, it remained vital and modernized to meet the nation's evolving needs.

Voices From the Rails: Stories of Sacrifice and Survival

To truly appreciate the human stories behind the Canadian Pacific Railway, its worth while taking a look at evidence left by those who lived through this transformative era. Personal accounts, newspaper articles, and historical records can vividly portray the sacrifices, struggles, and triumphs of the diverse people whose lives were forever changed by the railway's construction and operation.

Testimony of a Chinese Laborer on the CPR

In the heart of the Canadian Rockies, a Chinese laborer, known only as Li Wei, worked tirelessly alongside hundreds of his fellow countrymen. The job was grueling: chiseling through solid rock, laying down dynamite, and then retreating to safety before the blast. Many, like Li Wei, lived in constant fear of accidents. He recalled, "Men would be lowered down cliffs with dynamite, and not all of them came back up." The workers, paid less than their white counterparts, endured long hours with little rest.

Their camps were rudimentary, often nothing more than tents, with scant protection against the harsh elements. Li Wei described the brutal winters, where frostbite was common and the risk of avalanches ever-present. Despite their essential contribution to the railway, the Chinese workers faced discrimination and were often treated as expendable. Li Wei remembered the camaraderie among the workers, a bond forged in hardship, but also the overwhelming sense of isolation and longing for home. Letters from loved ones were rare, and many wondered if they would ever see their families again. The dangers they faced, coupled with the unforgiving landscape, made the work on the CPR a perilous endeavor, one that claimed many lives.

Testimony of a Scottish Immigrant Worker

John MacLeod, a Scottish immigrant, arrived in Canada with dreams of a better life, only to find himself working on the Canadian Pacific Railway in one of the most remote and challenging sections. His days were spent battling the harsh Canadian wilderness. "The work was backbreaking," he wrote in a letter to his brother back in Scotland. "Every day, we moved tons of earth, laid miles of track, and cleared trees as tall as the sky itself."

The weather was one of the biggest challenges; summers were blistering hot, and winters were bone-chilling cold. The men worked through it all, driven by the promise of a steady wage and the hope of land ownership. Yet, the isolation weighed heavily on John. "We are miles from the nearest town, and the only company we have are the men we work with," he wrote. The work camps were basic, with little in the way of comfort. Disease was a constant threat, with outbreaks of scurvy and smallpox decimating the workforce. Despite the hardships, John held onto his dreams, but he knew that many of his fellow workers would not survive to see theirs realized. The toll on their bodies and spirits was immense, a high price to pay for progress.

Government Inspector's Report on CPR Conditions

A government inspector, tasked with reporting on the conditions of the workers building the CPR, documented his findings with a sense of urgency. The inspector, known as James Caldwell, traveled to some of the most remote and perilous sections of the railway, including the Fraser Canyon and the Rocky Mountains. His report detailed the treacherous working conditions that the men, particularly the Chinese laborers, faced daily. "The men are employed in tasks that would challenge even the most seasoned of workers," Caldwell wrote. He noted the frequent accidents, particularly those involving explosives. "It is not uncommon to see men maimed by premature detonations or crushed by falling rock."

The living conditions in the camps were another point of concern. Caldwell observed that the shelters provided little protection against the elements, and the diet was poor, often leading to outbreaks of scurvy. "The men subsist on a diet of salted meat and hardtack, with little in the way of fresh produce," he reported. Despite these conditions, Caldwell noted the resilience of the workers, many of whom continued out of necessity, driven by the hope of a better future. His report, while intended to spur improvements, also served as a stark reminder of the human cost of the railway's construction.

Newspaper Account of a CPR Accident

The Victoria Daily Colonist published a brief yet sobering account of an accident on the Canadian Pacific Railway that claimed the lives of several workers. The article, dated 1884, recounted a rockslide that occurred in the Fraser Canyon, a section of the railway known for its perilous terrain. "Tragedy struck yesterday as a rockslide buried a group of men working on the new railway line," the report began. The newspaper provided a factual account, listing the number of fatalities and the efforts made to recover the bodies. "The men, working tirelessly to carve a path through the mountains, were caught off guard as the earth gave way above them," it described. The article highlighted the dangers inherent in the construction, noting that this was not the first, nor likely the last, such incident. "The work on the CPR is not for the faint of heart," the article concluded. It briefly mentioned the bravery of the workers but focused more on the progress of the railway than the human lives lost.

This detached tone was common in the media of the time, reflecting the era's prioritization of industrial progress over individual suffering. Yet, even in its brevity, the article conveyed the stark reality that the railway was being built on the backs—and sometimes the graves—of those who labored on it.In conclusion, the voices from the rails offer powerful testaments to the human dimensions of the Canadian Pacific Railway's history. Through their stories of hardship, resilience, and hope, we're reminded that the railway's legacy extends far beyond economic and political impact. It's a story of people –

workers who toiled in unforgiving conditions, families seeking new beginnings, and communities transformed by the railway's presence.

Chapter 7: The Great War and The Roaring Twenties

Battlefronts and Homefronts: A Nation Transformed

As the 1900s dawned, Canada found itself pulled between two contrasting realities - the bloody battlefields of World War I and the glittering promise of the Roaring Twenties. Our brave soldiers faced the horrors of trench warfare in Europe. But at home, the postwar years brought sweeping social, cultural, and economic changes as Canada emerged from war into an era of modernity.

To understand this profound transformation, we must examine how these two worlds intertwined. The Great War devastated the nation's psyche. Nearly 61,000 Canadians perished, and countless more returned home wounded physically and psychologically. The war effort touched every facet of society - from farmers and factory workers supplying the front, to grieving families mourning lost sons.

Yet amidst that turmoil, a spirit of progress was taking root. The Roaring Twenties challenged traditions and reshaped society. Emboldened by their wartime roles, women demanded more rights. In 1918, Canadian women won the right to vote federally after the suffragette movement gained momentum.

Urbanization and industrialization boomed in the 1920s as people flocked from rural areas to cities seeking jobs. Mass production and consumerism transformed the economy, birthing a new middle class. With disposable income, Canadians embraced modern life's trappings - cars, radios, movies, and jazz.

Through it all, Canadians showed remarkable resilience. They mourned losses, celebrated triumphs, and persevered through adversity.

The war tested the nation's mettle and found it strong. The Twenties unleashed innovation that would propel Canada forward.

This era reflects Canada's broader duality - a vast nation yet sparsely populated, fiercely independent yet tied to Britain, a mosaic of cultures united by purpose. War and the Roaring Twenties highlighted tensions between tradition and modernity, sacrifice and celebration, unity and diversity.

But it was Canada's ability to navigate these contradictions that allowed it to emerge stronger. The war forged a common identity. The Twenties brought progress. A nation came of age, learning to adapt and thrive amidst challenges.

Echoes of Valor: Who Were the Canadian Forces?

To truly understand how greatly Canadians contributed and sacrificed during World War I, we must first look at the brave individuals who made up the Canadian Forces. They were not mere statistics or nameless soldiers, but people with unique stories, backgrounds, and motivations. By exploring who they were, we gain a deeper appreciation for the courage and diversity of this remarkable generation.

The term "Canadian Forces" might seem to represent a homogeneous group, but that could not be further from the truth. Its men and women came from all walks of life, reflecting Canada's rich societal tapestry. Farmers, factory workers, students, and professionals - they all left their ordinary lives behind to answer the call of duty.

Some were "eager volunteers" who rushed to enlist early in the war, fueled by patriotism and a thirst for adventure. Often young and idealistic, they dreamed of glory and believed in the righteousness of their cause, unaware of the true horrors awaiting them on Europe's battlefields.

Others were "conscripted soldiers," brought involuntarily into the ranks as casualties mounted and the government implemented conscription. Many were older with families, thrust into the fray against their will. Yet despite their initial reluctance, numerous conscripts served with great distinction and bravery, proving courage knows no bounds.

The Canadian Forces also included "Indigenous warriors" - First Nations, Métis, and Inuit soldiers who fought alongside non-Indigenous comrades.

Vital too were the "immigrant soldiers" who had come to Canada seeking a better life only to find themselves embroiled in global conflict. They fought not just for their adopted country but for hope of a brighter future for their families, their sacrifices a testament to immigrant strength and Canada's multicultural fabric.

We cannot forget the "women in service" - nurses, ambulance drivers, and support staff who faced danger working tirelessly near the front lines. Their compassion and resilience tending to the wounded were a beacon of hope, reminding us bravery transcends gender.

Understanding these diverse groups within the Canadian Forces is key to appreciating Canada's full involvement. Each brought unique experiences, fears, and aspirations, creating a mosaic of courage and sacrifice that shaped the nation's identity.

The Echo of the Guns: Canada's Legacy of the Great War

Have you ever thought about how much World War I shaped Canada's national identity? As we consider Canada's involvement in the Great war our minds turn to the unimaginable losses Canadians suffered and their heroic valor displayed on the battlefield. Yet their sacrifices and achievements in the face of adversity transformed Canada profoundly. From the ashes of the battlefield, our nation emerged stronger, more united, and forever marked by the wartime experience.

The Great War left an enduring legacy that shaped our nation's policies, culture, pride, and place on the world stage for generations.

The scars ran deep, but so did the sense of national purpose and identity forged in the crucible of conflict. A legacy is something handed down from the past - a long-lasting impact or consequence. For Canada, the Great War's legacy spans the myriad ways the war effort and aftermath influenced our young nation's trajectory in the 20th century and beyond.

This multifaceted legacy includes the war's impact on Canada's international standing and reputation. The valor displayed by Canadian troops in battles like Vimy Ridge and Passchendaele earned our nation newfound respect globally. Vimy Ridge, in particular, has been immortalized as a pivotal moment in Canadian history – often described as the "birth of a nation." It was the first time all four Canadian divisions fought together as a cohesive unit, demonstrating exceptional bravery, strategic prowess, and determination. This victory was not just a military success; it was symbolic of Canada's emergence from the shadow of Britain and its assertion as an independent nation with its own identity.

By the war's end, Canada had not only contributed significantly to the Allied victory but had also gained a voice on the international stage. No longer just a British colony, Canada began asserting its distinct identity. The Canadian Corps' achievements fostered a sense of pride and unity back home, setting the stage for greater autonomy in international affairs. This was cemented when Canada signed the Treaty of Versailles independently and joined the League of Nations as an autonomous country, marking a major step towards full nationhood.

The war also accelerated Canada's political evolution. Total war demanded unprecedented federal powers and a more activist state. The introduction of income tax as a "temporary" measure, for example, reflected the government's need to finance the war effort. Though intended as a short-term solution, income tax became a permanent fixture in Canadian life, illustrating how the war reshaped the relationship between the government and its citizens.

The 1917 conscription crisis further tested national unity, exposing deep divisions between English and French Canadians. While many English-speaking Canadians supported conscription as a necessary measure to sustain the war effort, many French Canadians opposed it, feeling disconnected from Britain's imperial ambitions. The crisis strained relations between the two linguistic communities, a tension that reverberated throughout the 20th century. Despite these challenges, the war fostered a greater sense of national cohesion as Canadians of diverse backgrounds rallied around the common cause.

Socially and culturally, the legacy ran just as deep. The war shaped a generation – the deeply affected WWI veteran community and grieving families of over 60,000 dead Canadians. The scars were psychological as well as physical. The sheer scale of loss and suffering altered the fabric of Canadian society. The 1920s saw a rise in conservative Christianity as the bereaved sought solace, and postwar disillusionment gave rise to artistic movements that grappled with the trauma of war.

Memorials and Remembrance Day ceremonies became fixtures across Canada, testaments to loss and grief. Nearly every town and city erected monuments to honor the fallen, and the image of the soldier became a powerful symbol of sacrifice and national pride. The war also transformed Canadian literature, art, and culture, with works by authors like John McCrae, who penned the famous war poem "In Flanders Fields," resonating deeply with the national consciousness.

Yet the war also fostered Canadian nationalism and pride. Achievements like Vimy became central to our emerging national mythology. A generation saw the war through the lens of valor and sacrifice for a noble cause, shaping how Canadians viewed themselves and their place globally. The war marked a turning point in Canada's cultural identity, reinforcing a sense of independence and self-confidence that had been gradually developing since Confederation.

Economically, the war spurred growth in Canadian industry and an era of material prosperity for some with the Roaring Twenties. The demands of war production boosted sectors like manufacturing and mining, leading to economic expansion. Women, who had entered the workforce in unprecedented numbers during the war, laid the groundwork for future social change and gender equality movements.

But transitioning to a peacetime economy wasn't seamless. The postwar recession triggered economic dislocation, labor unrest, and social upheaval. Strikes became more common as workers demanded better wages and working conditions, emboldened by the sacrifices they had made during the war. The Winnipeg General Strike of 1919, one of the largest strikes in Canadian history, underscored the tensions between labor and capital that the war had exacerbated.

The war's origins in European power politics also sparked a growing desire in Canada to avoid foreign entanglements in the interwar years. There was also disillusionment with war itself, particularly among veterans who experienced its horrors firsthand. The memory of the war contributed to Canada's cautious approach to foreign policy, reflected in its initial reluctance to become involved in World War II. The Great War cast a long shadow that shaped Canada's response to the next global conflict in 1939 and influenced its commitment to peacekeeping in later decades.

Canada's efforts in peacekeeping missions and international diplomacy throughout the 20th century can be seen as an extension of the lessons learned from the Great War. The desire to prevent future conflicts and promote global stability became a key aspect of Canada's identity on the world stage, a direct outgrowth of the wartime experiences and sacrifices that had shaped the nation.

For individual Canadian families, the legacy took the form of lost loved ones, shattered dreams, and cherished memories passed down through generations as reminders of the human toll and intimate impact on countless lives. The war profoundly affected every corner of the country, leaving few untouched by its consequences. The stories of those who served and those who waited anxiously at home became part of the national narrative, woven into the fabric of Canadian society.

The Great War's legacy isn't frozen in time. Each generation grapples with its meaning anew. Historians explore its manifold impacts; poets, artists, and filmmakers reinterpret its significance for contemporary audiences. The act of remembrance itself evolves as part of the legacy, ensuring that the sacrifices and lessons of the past continue to resonate in the present.

Canada emerged from the Great War a different nation – more confident, more assertive, and more aware of its place in the world. The war was a crucible that forged Canada's identity and set it on a course that would shape its future. As we remember the sacrifices and triumphs of those who served, we recognize that the legacy of the Great War is not just a story of the past, but a vital part of who we are today.

Jazz, Flappers, and the Spirit of Rebellion

The clock struck midnight on January 16, 1920, marking a significant event - the United States ratified the 18th Amendment, ushering in the era of Prohibition. This momentous decision had far-reaching consequences beyond American borders, reaching their northern neighbors in Canada. Although selling and consuming alcohol remained legal in Canada, the country could not escape the cultural shockwaves rippling from the speakeasies and dance halls south of the border. The Roaring Twenties had arrived, unleashing a tidal wave of social, artistic, and cultural transformations that forever altered the fabric of Canadian society.

To fully grasp the impact of this transformative decade, we must revisit its beginnings. The earliest roots of Canada's cultural revolution in the 1920s trace back to the aftermath of World War I. Soldiers returning from European battlefields brought a newfound sense of disillusionment and a desire to break free from traditional societal constraints. Women, too, had tasted independence during the war years, taking on new roles in the workforce and challenging long-held gender norms.

Against this backdrop, a new cultural movement took shape. In the smoky jazz clubs of Montreal and Toronto, young people gathered to dance to the syncopated rhythms of legends like Duke Ellington and Louis Armstrong. The music was fast, frenetic, and unlike anything before – a soundtrack for a generation eager to throw off the shackles of the past and embrace a liberated way of life.

But jazz was only the beginning. As the decade unfolded, a new breed of young women known as "flappers" emerged. With their bobbed hair, short skirts, and devil-may-care attitudes, these women embodied the rebellious spirit of the age. They smoked cigarettes, drove fast cars, and danced the night away in underground speakeasies. Their influence on fashion, attitudes, and social norms cannot be overstated.

Of course, not everyone embraced these changes. Many older Canadians viewed the flapper lifestyle as a threat to traditional values and morality. Religious leaders and conservative politicians railed against the excesses of the younger generation, warning of the dangers of jazz music, alcohol, and loose morals.

As the 1920s wore on, the cultural revolution spread from cities to other parts of the country. On the Prairies, farmers struggling with drought and economic hardship found solace in the upbeat sounds of country music. In the Maritimes, traditional Celtic music blended with African-American blues to create a unique regional sound. And in Quebec, a new generation of French-Canadian artists and writers emerged, eager to assert their cultural identity in the face of English-Canadian domination.

Perhaps the most enduring legacy of the Roaring Twenties in Canada was the way it challenged traditional notions of identity and belonging. For the first time, Canadians began to see themselves not just as British subjects or members of local communities, but as part of a larger, more diverse national identity. The influx of immigrants from Europe and elsewhere brought new ideas, customs, and perspectives to the country, enriching its cultural landscape in unimaginable ways just decades earlier.

Of course, the Roaring Twenties were not without challenges and contradictions. The same forces that fueled cultural innovation and social progress also stoked economic inequality, political instability, and racial tensions. The stock market crash of 1929 and the subsequent Great Depression brought the era to a crashing halt, leaving many Canadians struggling to make ends meet.

Despite these challenges, the spirit of rebellion and innovation that defined the 1920s endured. The cultural and social changes that took root during this transformative decade continued shaping Canadian society for generations. From modern feminism's rise to the emergence of new artistic expressions, the Roaring Twenties' legacy remains felt today.

Looking back, the Roaring Twenties were a time of both great promise and great peril. They represented a moment when Canada stood on the brink of a new era, poised between the old world and the new. While the path forward was not always clear, one thing was certain: the country would never be the same again.

Votes for Women: The Fight for Suffrage

In 19th-century Canada, the right to vote was primarily reserved for men. But in an era of change and progress, a growing number of women's voices began demanding equality at the ballot box. Their fight would span generations, requiring immense sacrifice and resilience in the face of bitter opposition. This is the story of how Canadian women won their right to vote.

The roots of the suffrage movement stretch back to the 1870s. Early pioneers like Dr. Emily Howard Stowe and her daughter, Dr. Augusta Stowe-Gullen, advocated for women's enfranchisement. Other trailblazers soon joined them, such as Nellie McClung, Louise McKinney, Henrietta Muir Edwards, Emily Murphy, and Irene Parlby - the Famous Five who led the suffrage charge in the early 20th century.

These women faced a daunting challenge. At that time, many viewed politics as strictly for men. They argued women lacked the intelligence, rationality, and independence to vote responsibly. Opponents claimed granting women suffrage would upend traditional gender roles, destabilize families, and even threaten the nation's moral fabric. Undeterred, suffragists pushed back, insisting that denying half the population a political voice was unfair and undemocratic.

To make their case, the suffragists used various tactics. They wrote editorials, circulated petitions, held rallies and demonstrations. The Famous Five traveled across the country, giving rousing speeches. Their wit and eloquence gradually swayed public opinion. In 1916, they helped make Manitoba the first province to grant some women the vote. But suffragists knew true victory required change at the federal level.

Their opportunity came with WWI. As thousands of Canadian men shipped off to fight, women stepped up on the home front. They worked in munitions factories, volunteered as nurses, and kept the economy running. Their vital contributions shattered stereotypes about female fragility and incompetence. Suffragists argued: How could a nation deny rights to the very women whose labor and sacrifice sustained it during wartime?

In 1917, the federal government yielded to pressure, granting the vote to women serving in the military or related to servicemen. It was an important first step but still excluded most women. Suffragists continued fighting, and in 1918, Canada passed a law enfranchising women over 21. It was a stunning victory decades in the making.

The impact was immediate and profound. In 1921, Agnes Macphail became Parliament's first elected woman. Others soon followed, advocating issues like maternal health, minimum wage, and old age pensions. Women's suffrage transformed Canadian politics to be more responsive to all citizens' concerns.

Of course, the victory remained incomplete. Indigenous women, along with Inuit and status Indians, remained disenfranchised until 1960.

So what lessons can we draw from the suffragists' struggle? First, they demonstrated the power of committed citizen action to drive change against entrenched opposition. Through tireless organizing, skillful advocacy, and moral persuasion, these women transformed the political landscape, with effects still felt today.

Chapter 8: Depression and Dust

How Did They Endure?

The Great Depression and the Dust Bowl of late 1929 and into the 1930s tested the resilience of Canadians like never before. As the economy crumbled and severe dust storms ravaged the Prairies, our ancestors found themselves facing hardships we can scarcely imagine today.

During those dark times, joblessness soared, and businesses collapsed. Poverty became an inescapable reality for many families. Farmers watched helplessly as their crops withered away amidst the choking dust. City dwellers lined up at soup kitchens, grappling with the indignity of having nothing. It was a time of immense psychological toll, where stress, uncertainty and hopelessness became a way of life.

But Canadians refused to surrender. Instead of waiting for someone else to save them, they took matters into their own hands. They adapted old technologies, creating innovative solutions like the "Bennett buggy" – a horse-drawn car that kept them mobile despite lacking gas or repairs. The government established relief camps, providing work, shelter, and a small wage for those who had nowhere else to turn.

Above all, communities came together, sharing what little they had. Neighbors helped neighbors, whether it was fixing a roof, planting a garden, or simply offering an ear to listen. In this spirit of cooperation and mutual aid, the fabric of society held firm against the greatest of odds.

A Tale of Two Canadas: Prosperity and Poverty

As Saskatchewan's farming families struggled through the economic and environmental devastation of the Great Depression, urban centers like Toronto and Montreal faced a remarkably different reality. The previous decade's economic boom spurred industrial work that buoyed these cities, making them seem worlds apart from the desolate, dusty prairies.

The 1920s ushered in an era of prosperity and growth for Toronto. The city's population surged as immigrants and rural Canadians flocked to the burgeoning metropolis, drawn by the promise of factory jobs and a better life. Skyscrapers pierced the skyline, testifying to the thriving economy and age of optimism.

But as the Great Depression set in, cracks appeared in Toronto's veneer of invincibility. Factories slowed production or closed entirely, leaving thousands jobless. Breadlines snaked through city streets, starkly contrasting the glittering shop windows and bustling cafes that characterized the city just years earlier.

Yet Toronto's industrial base buffered it against the worst ravages. While no one escaped unscathed, the city's diversified economy - with its mix of manufacturing, finance, and commerce - proved more resilient than the prairie provinces' reliance on agriculture.

Montreal experienced a similar story. Its port, a hub of international trade, had fueled an economic boom in the 1920s. Factories hummed with activity, churning out textiles, machinery, and consumer goods. The vibrant cultural scene, with jazz clubs and art galleries, seemed to embody the spirit of the age.

But Montreal could not escape the Depression's toll. As global trade slowed and demand for manufactured goods plummeted, factories laid off workers en masse. The once-thriving port became a ghost town, with idle ships at their berths.

Yet the city's economic diversity provided some protection. While factories struggled, Montreal's role as a financial and commercial center helped sustain economic activity. Its tight-knit neighborhoods, with strong social networks and community organizations, provided vital support for those hit hardest.

In both cities, the Depression sparked an outpouring of community support and innovation. Wealthy industrialists and ordinary citizens donated to relief efforts, establishing soup kitchens and homeless shelters. Artists and intellectuals raised awareness and boosted morale, staging benefit concerts and creating public art.

Most importantly, the crisis fostered a renewed sense of solidarity and social responsibility. Recognizing no one was immune to fortune's vagaries, city dwellers banded together to help neighbors in need. This spirit of community, born of shared hardship, left a lasting mark on Canada's urban centers.

For all their resilience, however, Toronto and Montreal's experiences differed starkly from the unrelenting desperation faced by rural Saskatchewan communities. While urban dwellers grappled with unemployment and poverty, they were spared the environmental catastrophe that compounded the prairies' economic woes.

In Saskatchewan, drought turned fertile fields to dust bowls, leaving farming families not just economically destitute, but literally unable to feed themselves. The land that sustained generations became a barren wasteland, offering no respite from the economic storm.

This contrast - between the hardship all Canadians faced and the particularly brutal prairie circumstances - underscores the complexity of this chapter in Canadian history. It reveals a nation grappling with a crisis that, while universal, played out starkly differently across diverse regions and communities.

From Despair to Hope: The Birth of Social Welfare

The Great Depression ravaged Canada in the 1930s, leaving a trail of shattered dreams and broken lives. Canadians grappled with an unprecedented economic crisis from coast to coast. Unemployment skyrocketed, poverty was widespread, and despair filled the air.

It became clear the old ways of handling hard times wouldn't suffice. The Depression's scale and severity demanded a bold new approach recognizing the government's duty to protect citizens during crises. From the depths of despair, the seeds of Canada's modern social welfare system were planted.

The problem staggered in scope and complexity. At its 1933 peak, one in five Canadians depended on government relief. Silent, empty factories once bustled in Toronto and Montreal, while bread lines stretched for blocks. On the prairies, drought and plunging wheat prices left farming families destitute as their livelihoods turned to dust.

The human toll was immeasurable. Families separated as men rode the rails searching for work. Children went hungry, their growth stunted by malnutrition. With no safety net, the elderly and infirm were extremely vulnerable. As the crisis dragged on endlessly, hope faded into grim resignation.

Against this backdrop, the government took tentative steps toward a more active welfare role. In 1935, PM R.B. Bennett's Conservatives introduced Canada's first national unemployment insurance program, though limited and ruled unconstitutional. It marked a crucial shift – acknowledging the government's duty to protect citizens from market forces.

Under Mackenzie King's Liberals, Canada's welfare system truly took shape. King, once opposed to intervention, saw it as necessary facing the Depression's toll. "If we can mobilize wealth for destruction, it is unthinkable our people cannot also mobilize to conquer poverty and unemployment," he declared.

King's government introduced landmark measures laying the foundation for today's safety net. The 1940 Unemployment Insurance Act established a national program providing temporary support for jobless workers. The 1944 Family Allowances Act provided monthly payments to families with children, ensuring no child went hungry.

And the Old Age Pensions Act expanded, offering security for the elderly.

These groundbreaking measures faced challenges. Unemployment insurance initially excluded many, like women and seasonal workers. Some criticized family allowance as overreach. And while improved, the old age pension still left many seniors in poverty.

Despite limitations, these welfare measures profoundly impacted millions of Depression-stricken Canadians. They provided a vital lifeline, alleviating the worst suffering and offering hope. Most importantly, they fundamentally shifted the government-citizen relationship, recognizing the state's role in ensuring all Canadians' wellbeing.

Other solutions proposed more radical economic restructuring, blaming capitalism for the Depression. Others called for old laissez-faire policies, insisting intervention would worsen matters. But the moderate reform path won, paving the way for Canada's modern welfare system.

The Depression-era reforms still impact us today. Employment Insurance remains a cornerstone safety net. Family allowance evolved into the Canada Child Benefit supporting millions of families. And the old age pension expanded, ensuring seniors' dignity and security.

Canada's welfare birth arose from despair and hardship, forged in the Depression's crucible. But it also sprang from hope and belief in human dignity. Looking back, we're reminded of that belief's enduring power and Canadians' incredible resilience.

Ultimately, Canada's Depression response story triumphs over adversity, of hope countering despair. It reminds us of coming together in crises, supporting each other through darkness. And it inspires building a more just, compassionate, equitable society for all Canadians.

Chronicles of Resilience: A Timeline

The Great Depression and Dust Bowl of the 1930s tested the resilience and spirit of Canada. This timeline traces the key events, policy changes, and community actions that shaped the nation's journey through that difficult decade. It reveals the strength and determination of Canadians in the face of hardship and despair.

In 1929, the stock market crash on Black Thursday rocked the global economy and marked the start of the Great Depression. Canadian exports plummeted as worldwide demand dried up, leading to mass layoffs and widespread unemployment.

In 1930, Prime Minister R.B. Bennett's Conservatives took power, pledging to tackle the crisis. Severe drought hit the Prairies, compounding economic troubles with environmental devastation. The Dust Bowl years began as the first dust storms swept across, stripping away precious topsoil and destroying crops.

Unemployment peaked at around 27% in 1931. The government introduced limited aid for the jobless and farmers, but it proved insufficient. The Prairie Farm Rehabilitation Administration (PFRA) was created to help farmers adapt to drought and prevent soil erosion.

The Dust Bowl intensified in 1932, with more frequent, severe dust storms forcing thousands to abandon their land. The "Bennett Buggy" – a car pulled by horses – became a symbol of the hard times. The Co-operative Commonwealth Federation (CCF) was formed, advocating economic reforms and social welfare.

In 1933, unemployment reached alarming levels. The government set up work camps that provided basic shelter and food for unemployed men in exchange for labor.

1934 saw the establishment of the Bank of Canada, a key institution for stabilizing the economy. The Dust Bowl reached its worst point that summer, with rock-bottom crop yields.

The 1935 On-to-Ottawa Trek, a protest by unemployed workers, ended in violent clashes with the RCMP in Regina. This event galvanized public opinion against the government's response to the crisis. Later that year, W.L.M. King's Liberals defeated Bennett, promising more interventionist policies.

The Wheat Board was formed in 1935 to stabilize wheat prices for struggling Prairie farmers. Rain began to ease the Dust Bowl in 1937, but recovery took years. Local groups like Saskatoon's Ladies Welfare League ran kitchens and distributed clothing to those in need.

In 1938, the National Housing Act provided loans for construction to spur economic recovery. Riots erupted in Vancouver over unemployment, reflecting the ongoing social unrest.

Canada joined WWII in 1939 after Germany invaded Poland, shifting the economic and political focus. Wartime production lifted the nation out of the Depression as factories reopened and jobs returned. Drought relief efforts also helped stabilize agriculture.

This timeline shows how economic, environmental, political, and social forces shaped Canada's Depression experience. It highlights the suffering endured by millions but also the resilience, innovation, and solidarity that emerged in response.

Voices From the Shadows: Evidence of Endurance

The Great Depression of the 1930s brought unprecedented hardship to Canadians, testing the nation's resilience and fortitude. To understand this crisis, it is crucial to examine personal letters, government records, and newspaper articles from that era, which provide a nuanced view of how individuals and communities responded to despair and sought recovery.

The economic collapse following the 1929 stock market crash devastated Canadian industries, leading to widespread unemployment and poverty. In the Prairies, the Dust Bowl compounded these problems, as severe drought and dust storms ruined crops and forced many families off their land.

Despite these challenges, Canadians demonstrated remarkable resilience and unity. Personal letters, like one from a Saskatchewan farmer in 1934, reveal how communities banded together to share resources and support each other during hard times. This spirit of solidarity was evident across the country, as grassroots organizations, mutual aid societies, and self-help groups provided essential services.

The government's response evolved over the decade. Initially criticized as inadequate, R.B. Bennett's administration took steps like creating the Prairie Farm Rehabilitation Administration (PFRA) to help farmers combat drought. Later, under Mackenzie King's leadership, more substantial interventions were introduced, such as unemployment insurance and housing programs that laid the groundwork for Canada's modern social safety net.

Newspaper articles from the era capture the public discourse, highlighting both the desperation and resilience of Canadians. While headlines reflected the widespread suffering, they also celebrated acts of kindness, ingenuity, and perseverance that helped sustain communities.

However, not all Canadians experienced the Depression equally. Indigenous communities, already marginalized, often suffered disproportionately, and racial minorities like Chinese Canadians faced heightened discrimination and exclusion.

Overall, the Depression tested Canada's social fabric but also reinforced the importance of collective action and government intervention. The lessons of resilience and solidarity from the 1930s remain relevant today, offering inspiration for how to navigate contemporary challenges.

By studying the diverse experiences of Canadians during the Depression, we gain a deeper understanding of how to build resilient, inclusive societies capable of withstanding crises. The voices from that era remind us that even in the darkest times, unity and mutual support can help us overcome adversity.

Ten Steps Out of Darkness

The Great Depression and Dust Bowl of the 1930s brought unprecedented challenges to Canadians, but they refused to be defeated. Through solidarity, resilience, adaptation, and an unbreakable spirit, they navigated the worst economic and ecological crisis in modern history. Here are ten key ways Canadians responded to the hardship:

1. Mutual Aid and Support: Communities across Canada came together in profound acts of solidarity. Neighbors shared food, provided shelter, and organized grassroots relief efforts. Volunteer-run soup kitchens in cities fed thousands, while rural farmers worked together to replant fields destroyed by dust storms. This community spirit was crucial in sustaining Canadians through the worst times.

2. Adapting Farming Practices: Farmers in the Prairies, hardest hit by the Dust Bowl, adapted their agricultural practices to combat drought and soil erosion. Techniques like contour plowing, strip farming, and planting tree shelter belts helped stabilize the land. Government programs, such as the Prairie Farm Rehabilitation Administration (PFRA), provided education and incentives for soil conservation.

3. Advocating for Relief and Reform: Canadians actively demanded government relief and reform through marches, rallies, and petitions. Grassroots movements like the Co-operative Commonwealth Federation (CCF) advocated for a more equitable society, pushing for policies that eventually led to the establishment of Canada's social safety net.

4. Maintaining Hope and Joy: Despite the hardships, Canadians found joy in simple pleasures. Families entertained themselves with card games, storytelling, and singalongs. This resilient optimism helped people endure and keep hope alive for better days.

5. Innovating and Starting Cooperatives: With traditional jobs scarce, many Canadians launched small businesses and cooperatives.

Workers pooled skills and resources to create new enterprises, while women sold homemade goods to support their families. These entrepreneurial efforts contributed to Canada's economic recovery.

6. Migration for Opportunity: Many Canadians migrated in search of work, especially from the Dust Bowl to other parts of the country. Although migration often meant family separations, it provided a lifeline for those seeking new opportunities and a fresh start.

7. Community Gardens and Shared Harvests: Community gardens, often called Relief Gardens, sprouted in vacant lots and schoolyards. These gardens provided essential food for families and fostered a sense of contribution and cooperation.

8. Work Relief Projects: As the Depression wore on, the government launched work relief projects that provided jobs building roads, bridges, and infrastructure. These projects offered employment and helped restore a sense of purpose to many who had been unemployed for years.

9. Pursuing Education and Skills Development: Education became a pathway to better opportunities, especially for young people. Some pursued higher learning or night classes that taught employable skills like typing and mechanics. While educational opportunities were limited, those who could access them found new doors opening.

10. Preserving Cultural Heritage: Cultural traditions provided strength and continuity during difficult times. Indigenous communities, despite facing severe challenges, maintained their ceremonies and cultural practices as acts of resilience. Similarly, other cultural groups preserved their languages, faiths, and traditions, which helped sustain their identities and communities.

These ten strategies – from economic innovation to cultural resilience – helped Canadians endure the Great Depression and Dust Bowl. The crisis demanded solidarity, sacrifice, and ceaseless effort, but in rising to those challenges, Canadians forged a stronger national identity.

The generation that came of age in the 1930s, who later fought in World War II and built the post-war order, learned indelible lessons about pulling together in hard times. Their experiences teach us that even in the darkest periods, solidarity, ingenuity, and hope can light the way forward.

Chapter 9: Canada in World War II

Who Stood Guard at Home?

Do you ever wonder who kept things running on the home front while battles raged overseas? This intriguing question opens a window into the lives of countless Canadians who contributed to the war effort without setting foot on the battlefield. These unsung heroes, from factory workers to farmers, played critical roles that helped secure victory abroad. Yet, their stories often remain untold. As we explore this fascinating chapter of history, we can uncover the resilience, sacrifice, and unwavering dedication of ordinary Canadians who stood guard at home.

Truly understanding Canada's wartime contribution requires appreciating the immense significance of the home front. While soldiers fought bravely abroad, their success depended on the vital support and resources provided by those who remained behind. The home front formed the very backbone of the war machine, supplying materials, food, and morale that fueled the fight for freedom. Without the tireless efforts of millions of Canadians on the domestic front, achieving victory would have been an impossible dream.

Those on the home front faced daunting, complex challenges. As able-bodied men enlisted, key industries and agriculture faced massive labor shortages. Women, previously relegated to domestic roles, suddenly found themselves thrust into the workforce, taking on jobs once exclusive to men. Factories had to rapidly retool to produce military equipment and supplies. Farmers raced to maximize their crop yields to feed troops and civilians alike. Citizens endured rationing, blackouts, and the constant fear of enemy attack, adding immense psychological strain.

Yet Canadians met these obstacles with remarkable resilience and ingenuity. Women proved more than capable of filling the void left by men, excelling as munitions workers, mechanics, and even pilots. Factories hummed nonstop, churning out ships, aircraft, uniforms, ammunition, and more. Farmers worked tirelessly to boost yields, often aided by prisoners of war or conscientious objectors assigned to agricultural labor. Countless volunteer organizations sprouted up in support, with citizens knitting socks, collecting scrap metal, and packing care packages to buoy morale on the front lines.

Beyond material contributions, the home front's morale-boosting efforts vitally sustained the fighting spirit of troops abroad. Letters, care packages, and home-baked treats from loved ones provided a tangible connection to life back in Canada, reminding soldiers their sacrifices mattered and they weren't forgotten. Communities rallied together, offering comfort and support to military families, fostering a shared sense of purpose amidst adversity.

These unsung heroes came from all walks of life, each playing their part. Every contribution, no matter how small, helped make victory possible. Though they didn't face battlefield dangers directly, their sacrifices and dedication proved no less vital. By keeping the home fires burning, they not only buttressed the war effort, but laid the foundation for the prosperous, peaceful nation we enjoy today.

So who stood guard at home during wartime? It was those tireless, dedicated Canadians whose stories deserve our utmost attention and respect. These unsung home front heroes, through their efforts and sacrifices, played a pivotal role shaping history and securing the very freedom we cherish. As we remember the bravery of those who fought abroad, we must also honor those who overcame immense challenges and kept the nation persevering on the domestic front – for their contributions proved equally indispensable in the noble cause of victory.

Juno Beach: D-Day's Canadian Heroes

On that misty June 6th morning in 1944, the tide of World War II turned. Allied forces launched history's largest amphibious assault—D-Day. Brave Canadian soldiers were among those storming Normandy's beaches to capture Juno. This study transports us back to that fateful day when meticulous planning, fierce combat, and incredible bravery marked Canada's pivotal invasion role that altered the war's course and shaped our world's future.

The task before the Canadians was immense. Juno Beach stretched with formidable German defenses—heavily fortified bunkers, machine-gun nests, and mines awaiting the approaching forces. The Normandy invasion's entire success hinged on capturing each beach. The determined Canadians would not let their Allies down. Battle-hardened from Italian campaigns, the 3rd Canadian Infantry Division and 2nd Canadian Armoured Brigade would spearhead the assault with support from the Royal Canadian Navy and Air Force.

Meticulous planning preceded the assault. Aerial reconnaissance provided invaluable intelligence on enemy positions, allowing strategists to develop a detailed attack plan. Practice landings honed the soldiers' skills while specialized equipment like the amphibious Duplex Drive tanks prepared to support infantry. Secrecy was paramount—the element of surprise could make the difference between victory and disaster. As H-Hour neared, tension mounted with the impending battle's palpable weight.

On that fateful morning, as landing crafts neared shore under artillery barrages, Canadians steeled themselves for the fight of their lives. Bullets whizzed and explosions rent the air. The surf ran red as soldiers disembarked, many never reaching the beach. Yet through chaos and carnage, Canadians pushed forward with grim determination, neutralizing enemy positions one by one. Juno's sands became a testament to their valor, each yard gained paid for with blood and sacrifice.

Despite casualties, Canadians persevered. Specialized Royal Canadian Engineer units worked tirelessly clearing obstacles and mines, enabling troops and vehicles to move inland. By afternoon, Canadians achieved their objectives, penetrating deeper into Normandy than any other Allied force. The price was steep—over 900 Canadians lost, countless more wounded. But their bravery and sacrifice opened the way.

Juno's capture was a turning point, a foothold allowing Allied forces to pour into Europe, marking Nazi Germany's beginning of the end. Canadian success showcased the power of training, teamwork, indomitable spirit, meticulous planning, specialized equipment, and above all, individual soldier courage. Juno's lessons resonate—the importance of adaptability, sacrificing for a greater cause, and unity's power facing adversity.

But Juno was more than strategic victory—it was profoundly human. Each storming soldier carried a nation's hopes and fears, each life lost a shattered dream. Canadians fought for a vision of freedom from tyranny, oppression, and war's spectre. Facing unimaginable odds and horrors, they found unknown reserves of courage and resilience within themselves.

Reflecting on June 6, 1944, we owe those that laid down their lives a profound debt. Their sacrifices, unwavering duty commitment, and belief in freedom's cause shaped today's world. Juno's blood-stained sands now silently tribute their heroism, sacred ground where the future was forged.

For those storming Juno, failure was not an option. They embarked with conviction their cause was just, their purpose noble. In combat's crucible, they forged a legacy enduring long after the last veteran passes. Theirs is ordinary people achieving extraordinary things, transformative courage and sacrifice's power.

Warriors and Guardians: Indigenous

Contributions

When World War II erupted in chaos and horror, Indigenous peoples of Canada and Allied nations faced conflicting realities. Many Indigenous men and women voluntarily enlisted, eager to serve their countries. They wanted to defend freedom and democracy against fascism and oppression. These Indigenous soldiers brought unique skills honed by generations of living close to the land - resilience, adaptability, marksmanship, and deep understanding of the natural world. Yet there was a bitter irony for some that served. For some fought for nations that at times oppressed, marginalized, and tried to remove their cultures and identities. Many grew up under the shadow of residential schools, forcibly separated from families and communities. Their languages and traditions were suppressed. They witnessed encroachment on their lands and erosion of rights and sovereignty. Even while donning their countries' uniforms, they carried scars and trauma from colonialism and racism.

This stark contrast between Indigenous veterans' valor and sacrifice and the injustices they faced at times at home is a critical but often overlooked aspect of the World War II narrative. It complicates the traditional heroic war story, revealing complexities and contradictions of the Indigenous experience during this pivotal time.

Indigenous service members played vital roles across all war theaters. In the Pacific, Navajo Code Talkers used their language to create an unbreakable code securing Allied victories. In Europe, snipers and scouts utilized tracking and survival skills to gather intelligence and eliminate targets. Indigenous women served as nurses, mechanics, and other essential roles. Their World War II service stories are living testaments to Indigenous peoples' courage, resilience, and determination against unimaginable odds. They challenge us to confront injustices shaping our nations' histories and work towards reconciliation and respect.

Rosie the Riveter, Meet Veronica Foster: Women at War

Dark storm clouds of World War II gathered on the horizon, posing an unprecedented crisis for Canadian society. Men were being called to fight overseas, leaving critical factory, office, and farm roles vacant. The very fabric of the nation was under threat as key industries risked grinding to a halt. Women, long confined to the domestic sphere, suddenly had an opportunity and a challenge. Could they step up and fill the void left by their fathers, brothers, and husbands? Could they keep the home fires burning while also fueling the war machine?

The problem's scale was immense. Thousands of positions needed filling across various sectors. Munitions factories required skilled hands to produce bullets and bombs for Allied forces. Farms needed tending to ensure a steady food supply for both the military and civilians. Clerical and administrative roles had to be filled to keep the government and businesses running smoothly. Without women's participation, Canada's war effort would be crippled, jeopardizing not just the nation but the entire Allied cause.

Inaction carried dire consequences. A lack of munitions could mean underequipped soldiers facing higher casualties. Food shortages could lead to rationing and unrest on the home front. Inadequate administrative support could cause chaos and confusion, undermining military strategy and planning. The war's very outcome hung in the balance, dependent on Canadian women's willingness and ability to mobilize.

The solution: a massive recruitment and training effort to bring women into the workforce. The government launched propaganda campaigns featuring iconic figures like Veronica Foster, the "Ronnie the Bren Gun Girl," encouraging women to take up industrial jobs. Rosie the Riveter's famous "We Can Do It!" slogan became a rallying cry, empowering women to see themselves as capable and vital contributors.

Employment offices matched women with suitable positions, and training programs equipped them with necessary skills.

Implementation faced challenges. Many men resisted women taking on "masculine" roles, and some workplaces struggled to accommodate female workers. Safety concerns, particularly in industrial settings, had to be addressed. Childcare facilities enabled mothers to work outside the home. Women navigated a delicate balance between traditional domestic duties and new roles as breadwinners and patriots.

Despite obstacles, the results were remarkable. By 1944, over one million Canadian women worked in the war effort. They welded, machined, and wired in factories. They took over farming duties, ensuring food supplies. They served in clerical and administrative positions, keeping government and industry functioning. Their contributions proved instrumental in Allied victories, from Normandy to the Pacific.

The Price of Peace: Canada's Economic Transformation

As Canada emerged from World War II, one fundamental question loomed: What would be the cost of peace? The war had exacted an immense toll through lost lives and expended resources. However, amidst the devastation, a surprising fact emerged - Canada's economy had undergone a remarkable transformation, paving the way for an unprecedented era of prosperity.

At its core, this economic transformation was a story of adaptation and resilience. Canada evolved rapidly from a nation reliant on agriculture and resource extraction into an industrial powerhouse. The war necessitated an all-hands-on-deck approach. Factories retooled for military production. Women flooded into the workforce. Government spending soared to unparalleled levels.

This wartime mobilization had far-reaching effects. It fueled once-languishing industries with insatiable demand for war materiel. Shipyards hummed with activity, producing a prodigious number of vessels from minesweepers to merchant ships. Aircraft factories sprouted up across the country, churning out thousands of planes for the Allied cause. The automotive sector underwent a breathtaking shift from civilian to military production.

The war years also transformed the relationship between government and the economy. Facing an existential threat, the state took on a larger role, directing resources, setting prices, and shaping production priorities. This wartime planning laid the groundwork for a more active government role in the postwar years, profoundly impacting Canada's economic trajectory.

Yet, even as the war raged, Canadians contemplated the postwar world. Would the wartime boom give way to a devastating bust, like after World War I? Policymakers and ordinary citizens pondered these questions.

Remarkably, the postwar years defied dire predictions, bringing a sustained economic boom instead of a recession. Pent-up consumer demand fueled by high wartime savings led to a consumption bonanza. Government investments in infrastructure, housing, and education laid foundations for long-term growth. Skills and technologies honed during the war found new civilian applications, driving productivity gains across industries.

The postwar boom brought challenges too. Demobilization raised the specter of mass unemployment as thousands of soldiers returned home seeking work. Inflation reared its head as price controls lifted. Transitioning from a wartime to peacetime economy required a delicate reallocation of resources as industries retooled again.

Despite obstacles, Canada's economic transformation proved remarkably durable. The postwar decades witnessed sustained growth, rising living standards, and a robust middle class emerged. This prosperity was not evenly distributed - indigenous communities faced systemic barriers and economic marginalization. Still, for many Canadians, the postwar era represented opportunity and upward mobility.

In many ways, Canada's wartime economic transformation shaped the nation we know today. The industrial capacity set the foundation for our modern manufacturing base. Active government economic management became a defining Canadian model. Social programs and investments like universal healthcare and accessible post-secondary education became societal cornerstones.

Timeline of Triumph: Canada's Path to Victory

Canada's journey through World War II was a defining moment in its history, reshaping its national identity and altering its global standing. This narrative highlights the pivotal events that shaped Canada's wartime experience and its future, from the early days of the conflict to the hard-fought victory.

On September 10, 1939, Canada officially entered the war, a week after Britain and France declared war on Germany following the invasion of Poland. As a member of the British Commonwealth, Canada was committed to the Allied cause under Prime Minister Mackenzie King, marking the beginning of nearly six years of transformation and struggle.

In December 1939, Canada launched the British Commonwealth Air Training Plan, an ambitious program that trained over 130,000 airmen from across the Commonwealth. Dubbed the "aerodrome of democracy," this initiative solidified Canada's reputation as a key player in the war effort.

The Battle of Britain in June 1940 saw Canadian fighter pilots join the fray, earning a legendary reputation for their bravery and skill. The Royal Canadian Air Force's contributions were instrumental in securing this crucial victory.

In December 1941, nearly 2,000 under-prepared Canadian soldiers faced a harsh reality during the defense of Hong Kong against the Japanese invasion. This battle marked Canada's first major engagement in the Pacific and underscored the war's brutal challenges.

The ill-fated Dieppe Raid on August 19, 1942, involving over 6,000 men, predominantly Canadians, was a costly endeavor. However, the lessons learned were invaluable for the planning of future amphibious assaults, including D-Day.

Throughout the war, Canada's contributions extended beyond the battlefield. At home, the economy shifted to wartime production, and women entered the workforce in unprecedented numbers, taking on crucial roles in industry and agriculture.

Yet, the costs were immense. Over 45,000 Canadians lost their lives, with many more wounded physically and mentally. The scars of battles like Dieppe and the Scheldt would linger long after the war ended.

Despite these sacrifices, Canada's war experience was marked by extraordinary acts of heroism and resilience. Figures like Major Paul Triquet, Ojibway sniper Francis Pegahmagabow, and Nova Scotian nurse Mona Parsons exemplified the courage that defined the nation's war effort.

World War II accelerated Canada's transformation from a rural, agricultural nation to an urban, industrial one. It also sowed the seeds of the social welfare state and forged a new Canadian identity, balancing ties to Britain with an emerging sense of nationhood.

As we commemorate the 75th anniversary of the war's end, we honor those who served and sacrificed while reflecting on the enduring legacy of this pivotal period in Canada's history.

Evidencing Valor: Canadian Bravery in the Field

During World War II, Canadian forces demonstrated extraordinary bravery and resilience on battlefields across the globe. From the skies over Britain to the beaches of Normandy, the rugged terrain of Italy to the fierce battles in the Rhineland, Canadian soldiers, sailors, and airmen faced daunting challenges with unwavering resolve and quiet determination. Their valor and sacrifice were instrumental in the Allied victory, leaving an indelible mark on Canada's history and national identity.

To fully appreciate the courage of Canadian servicemen and women, we must examine evidence such as military records, war diaries, and awarded honors. These tangible sources not only attest to their heroism but also offer a deeper understanding of the harrowing experiences they endured. An evidence-based analysis provides a vivid portrayal of the valor that defined Canada's war effort, paying tribute to those who served and sacrificed.

One compelling piece of evidence is the Victoria Cross, the highest military decoration awarded for valor against the enemy. During World War II, 16 Canadians received this prestigious honor, each representing an extraordinary act of courage and self-sacrifice. The meticulously documented stories of these recipients provide a glimpse into the bravery that characterized Canada's war experience.

Consider Major Paul Triquet, awarded the Victoria Cross for his actions at the Battle of Casa Berardi in Italy on December 14, 1943. His citation reads: "For most conspicuous gallantry...In a battle which lasted forty-eight hours, he was everywhere at the critical moments, both by day and night...The complete destruction of a German battalion was achieved, with heavy casualties to the enemy." Triquet's actions, corroborated by eyewitness accounts, exemplify the bravery and leadership shown by Canadian officers in battle. Despite heavy casualties and fierce resistance, Triquet rallied his men and led them to victory, embodying the spirit of Canadian valor.

War diaries of Canadian units also provide firsthand evidence of soldiers' bravery and sacrifice. The Queen's Own Rifles' diary chronicles their harrowing experience on D-Day, June 6, 1944: "The men were magnificent...There was no flinching or hesitation, and their discipline was of the highest order. The outstanding leadership and coolness displayed by the Officers and NCOs was an inspiration to all ranks. The bravery and self-sacrifice of all was beyond praise." This raw account, written amidst the chaos of Normandy, testifies to the courage and determination of Canadian soldiers. The vivid description of their discipline and leadership paints a powerful picture of the valor that echoes throughout Canadian military history.

Beyond the Victoria Cross and war diaries, the sheer number of honors awarded to Canadians speaks volumes. Over 18,000 military honors were given, including Distinguished Service Orders, Military Crosses, Distinguished Flying Crosses, and Military Medals. Each represents a story of courage, sacrifice, and devotion in the face of grave danger, reminding us of Canada's unwavering commitment to the Allied cause.

Consider Wing Commander R.W. McNair, who received the Distinguished Flying Cross for his actions during the Battle of Britain in 1940: "This officer has displayed outstanding gallantry and devotion to duty in leading his squadron into action...On several occasions, he has shot down enemy aircraft...During a very heavy battle over Dover on 19th August, Wing Commander McNair destroyed at least three of the enemy himself." McNair's bravery in the British skies, confirmed by his enemy kills, exemplifies the skill and courage of Canadian fighter pilots during pivotal stages of the air war. His leadership against the Luftwaffe onslaught stands as a shining example of Canadian valor.

While these honors recognize acts of bravery, countless more went unacknowledged amidst the chaos of war. The courage displayed by Canadians at Dieppe, Hong Kong, and the Scheldt, as they endured unimaginable hardships, remains a silent testament to the indomitable spirit that defined Canada's war effort.

Ultimately, the evidence of Canadian bravery speaks to a nation that punched above its weight on the global stage. Through their courage, sacrifice, and steadfast commitment to freedom, Canada's servicemen and women played a vital role in securing the Allied victory, forever altering their country's place in the world.

Ten Innovations That Shaped the War

World War II acted as a catalyst, driving scientists and engineers worldwide to push the boundaries of innovation. Canada played a crucial role beyond the battlefields, as Canadian ingenuity fueled groundbreaking advancements. These developments not only aided the Allied victory but also shaped the post-war world. From refining radar technology to improving penicillin production, Canadian inventions and discoveries left an indelible mark on science, medicine, and technology.

Let's explore ten Canadian innovations that emerged from the crucible of war and forever changed the world:

1. Radar Technology

Canada played a pivotal role in advancing radar technology. In 1939, the National Research Council established a top-secret project known as "Project Pimpernel." Led by physicist John Stuart Foster, the team developed the first successful Canadian radar set, the SW1C. This early warning system detected enemy aircraft and submarines, giving Allied forces a strategic edge. Canada's radar innovations, including the Plan Position Indicator display, revolutionized military surveillance and navigation, laying the groundwork for modern radar systems.

2. Penicillin Production

Canadian researchers at the Connaught Laboratories in Toronto made significant contributions to penicillin production. They developed a deep-tank fermentation method that increased yields, making mass production feasible. By 1944, Connaught was producing 30% of the penicillin used by Allied forces. This life-saving antibiotic saved countless lives during the war and marked a pivotal moment in the development of modern medicine.

3. Walkie-Talkie

Effective communication was critical on the battlefield. In 1942, Canadian engineer Donald Hings invented the portable two-way radio transceiver, commonly known as the walkie-talkie. Hings' CS-2 design allowed soldiers to communicate wirelessly over short distances, enhancing coordination and situational awareness. The walkie-talkie laid the foundation for modern mobile communication devices.

4. G-Suit

High-speed aviation posed challenges for pilots due to extreme G-forces, which could cause blackouts. Canadian researcher Wilbur Franks developed the G-suit to counteract this. The suit used water-filled bladders to apply counter-pressure to the pilot's body, preventing blood from pooling in the lower extremities. Franks' G-suit, first tested in 1940, became standard issue for Allied pilots, significantly enhancing their endurance and combat effectiveness.

5. Snowmobile

While not directly used in combat, the snowmobile's development had significant military and civilian applications. In 1937, Canadian inventor Joseph-Armand Bombardier designed the B7, a tracked vehicle for traversing snow. During the war, he adapted it to create the B1 snowmobile, which was used by the Canadian Army for winter transportation and patrol in northern regions. The B1's success led to larger, more versatile snowmobiles, revolutionizing winter travel.

6. Chemical Weapons Research

Despite the ban on chemical weapons after WWI, research continued to ensure preparedness against potential threats. Canadian scientists at the Suffield Experimental Station developed new chemical defense strategies, including the study of nerve agents like Tabun. While these chemical agents were not deployed during WWII, the research advanced scientific understanding of chemical warfare and contributed to modern defense and detection systems.

7. Computerized Artillery Predictor

Accurate artillery fire required complex calculations. Canadian physicist and mathematician Sanford A. Hogg developed the Predictor Automated Computer for Artillery (PACFA). PACFA used analog computers to rapidly calculate firing solutions, significantly improving artillery accuracy and efficiency. Hogg's invention foreshadowed the integration of computers into military systems and contributed to the digital revolution.

8. DUKW Amphibious Vehicle

The DUKW, or "Duck," was an amphibious vehicle designed to transport troops and supplies from ships to shore. Canadian manufacturer General Motors Canada played a crucial role in its development and production. The six-wheeled vehicle could navigate both land and water, making it invaluable for beach landings and river crossings. The DUKW's success influenced future amphibious vehicle designs and established Canada as a leader in specialized military vehicle production.

9. Nylon Parachutes

Before WWII, parachutes were made from silk, which was expensive and difficult to obtain. With the development of nylon, a new material became available. Canadian company Irvin Air Chute played a significant role in manufacturing and refining nylon parachutes. These parachutes were lighter, more compact, and more durable than silk, making them ideal for military use. The widespread adoption of nylon parachutes by Allied forces saved countless lives and reinforced Canada's reputation in parachute technology.

10. Polymer Innovations

During WWII, Canada faced material shortages that led to innovations in material science, though the introduction of polymer banknotes occurred later in history. However, wartime research into synthetic materials such as nylon and polymers paved the way for post-war advances in industries ranging from textiles to engineering.

These ten Canadian innovations exemplify how the country's scientific and technological prowess contributed to the Allied victory. From radar technology and penicillin production to the walkie-talkie and G-suit, Canadian ingenuity helped shape the course of the war and left a lasting impact on the world.

Canada's wartime innovations demonstrate the country's resilience, resourcefulness, and commitment to the Allied cause. Despite its relatively small size, Canada punched above its weight in scientific and technological contributions, earning a reputation as a nation of innovators and problem-solvers. The legacy of these innovations extends far beyond the conflict itself, influencing fields such as medicine, communication, transportation, and material science.

As we reflect on Canada's role in WWII, it is essential to recognize these technological advancements alongside the bravery and sacrifice of Canadian soldiers. These innovations serve as a testament to the power of human ingenuity in the face of adversity and the enduring impact of scientific progress on society. By celebrating these achievements, we honor the brilliant minds that helped shape history and inspire future generations to embrace innovation as a means of overcoming challenges and creating a better world.

Chapter 10: The Post-War Boom

Did Peace Pave the Way for Prosperity?

Can the horrors of global war lead to an era of peace and prosperity? This paradoxical question emerges when we explore Canadian history after World War II. The nation's transition from wartime chaos to post-war stability and growth was no coincidence—it showcased the resilience, innovation, and determination of the Canadian people.

Understanding this remarkable shift is crucial, as it offers valuable lessons for nations rebuilding after crises. By examining the factors behind Canada's success, we gain insight into the complex interplay of conflict, social reform, and economic growth. This knowledge remains relevant today as countries grapple with war, inequality, and the pursuit of prosperity.

World War II left Canada facing a daunting recovery. Lives were lost, infrastructure was damaged, and social and economic systems were disrupted. Yet, amid the rubble and grief, a spark of resilience and innovation began to glow. The war forced Canadians to adapt creatively and work together in unprecedented ways—qualities that would form the bedrock of future prosperity.

The transition from a wartime to a peacetime economy brought immense challenges. Demobilizing troops, reintegrating veterans, and shifting industrial output were major hurdles. Many feared the war's end would plunge the nation back into economic hardship akin to the Great Depression.

Yet Canada thrived in this critical period, emerging stronger than ever. The key lay in forward-thinking policies, social reforms, and a commitment to building a more equitable society. The government supported veterans, expanded access to education, and strengthened the social safety net. These moves eased the transition for those who served while paving the way for an inclusive, prosperous future.

One striking transformation was the explosive growth of the middle class. Before the war, society was divided between a wealthy elite and struggling masses. But in the following decades, rising wages, greater access to education, and the growth of new industries fueled a robust middle class. Prosperity was no longer limited to a select few.

Skeptics might argue that Canada's success was due to luck or good timing amidst a global economic boom. However, this overlooks the critical impact of deliberate policy choices and reforms. The government invested in infrastructure, education, and research, fostering innovation and entrepreneurship. It ensured that the benefits of growth were distributed widely through progressive taxation, social programs, and labor rights.

Canada's post-war experience offers valuable lessons for today. As conflict and inequality persist worldwide, the Canadian model provides a roadmap for building prosperity and equity. Prioritizing social reform, investing in human capital, and cultivating innovation can enable nations to emerge resilient from even the darkest times.

This path was not easy for Canada, which faced regional disparities, cultural tensions, and civil rights battles. Yet the nation confronted these challenges head-on, engaging in difficult conversations and working towards solutions that benefited all Canadians.

Reflecting on whether peace birthed prosperity, the answer is a resounding yes. But peace alone did not drive this transformation. It was a nation's tireless efforts to build a better future, harness past lessons, and create a more just, inclusive, and prosperous society.

The Laurier Memorial: A Symbol of Unity

In Canada's history, the Laurier Memorial stands as a powerful declaration of Indigenous rights and a call for justice. This pivotal document, presented in 1910 by the leaders of the Secwepemc, Okanagan, and Nlaka'pamux Nations, highlighted the injustices faced by Indigenous peoples in British Columbia. It serves as a testament to the ongoing struggle for recognition and fairness in a young nation grappling with the complexities of colonialism.

The summer of 1910 saw Indigenous leaders gather in Kamloops, British Columbia, to meet with Prime Minister Sir Wilfrid Laurier. As Canada built its identity as a nation, Indigenous peoples across the country faced tremendous challenges, from land dispossession to the erosion of their cultures. The Laurier Memorial, presented during this visit, was no ordinary petition. It was a profound statement that laid bare the impact of colonialism on Indigenous communities and demanded a just resolution.

For Laurier, the memorial represented an important moment of engagement with Indigenous leaders. However, despite the eloquence and urgency of the petition, there was no immediate or significant action taken in response. The memorial did not lead to direct negotiations or agreements but remains a key document that articulates the ongoing grievances of Indigenous peoples.

Later efforts, such as the McKenna-McBride Commission (1913-1916), sought to address some of the land issues raised by Indigenous leaders. However, these efforts were largely seen as inadequate and did not resolve the broader issues of land rights and sovereignty. The commission often reduced reserve lands, leading to further dissatisfaction among Indigenous communities.

Despite its limitations, the Laurier Memorial is a significant moment in Canadian history. It galvanized Indigenous leaders and remains a powerful reminder of the long struggle for justice and recognition in Canada. The memorial continues to inspire efforts toward reconciliation, serving as a symbol of the enduring demand for fairness and equality.

Boom or Bust: Comparing Post-War Eras

World War II left nations across the globe in ruins, forcing them to rebuild economies, societies, and national identities. Canada, like others, experienced a post-war boom that transformed its way of life. However, Canada's journey differed from the paths taken by other countries due to unique policies, cultural shifts, and economic strategies.

To understand Canada's boom in a global context, we must examine broader post-war trends. The war's end marked a pivotal moment as nations confronted a new world order. The United States and Soviet Union emerged as superpowers, entering a Cold War that shaped politics for decades. War-torn Europe began arduous reconstruction aided by the US Marshall Plan. Meanwhile, defeated Japan and Germany reinvented themselves under Allied occupation.

Against this backdrop, Canada's post-war boom stood as a remarkable success story. Like others, Canada emerged from war with renewed national purpose and aspirations for a better future. Its wartime economy had transformed, with industries retooled for military production and more women entering the workforce. As peace arrived, the challenge shifted to transitioning this mobilization into sustainable economic growth and prosperity.

One key factor distinguishing Canada's boom was government policy. The government stimulated growth and social welfare through measures like the Veterans Charter (benefits for returning soldiers), Family Allowance Act (financial aid for families with children), and major infrastructure projects modernizing transportation networks.

Canada's relationship with economic powerhouse United States was another unique aspect, presenting both opportunities and challenges. The US market and investment capital offered economic boosts, but close ties raised sovereignty concerns over potential American domination. To navigate this, successive governments pursued "quiet diplomacy" – maintaining US relations while asserting Canadian interests, exemplified by the 1965 Auto Pact creating a free automotive trade zone.

Culturally, the boom brought significant shifts as immigration from Europe and beyond increased, introducing new influences. The rising baby boom generation also profoundly impacted society, challenging traditional norms and values while demanding social and political change.

Unlike some comprehensive European welfare states, Canada adopted a more moderate social support approach balancing individual responsibility. Still, programs like universal healthcare and the Canada Pension Plan in the 1960s expanded the social safety net.

As a resource-rich nation, Canada had long exported raw commodities. Post-war, the government encouraged domestic processing and value-added production with mixed results. Alberta's petrochemical industry and Quebec's hydroelectric expansion succeeded, but resource dependency persisted with boom-and-bust challenges.

While many European countries nationalized industries, Canada maintained a market approach relying on private enterprise and foreign investment. This attracted capital and innovation but left vulnerabilities to global economic forces.

By the 1970s, Canada emerged prosperous with a high living standard, diverse economy, and strong global reputation. However, rapid change brought new tensions around environmental degradation, regional disparities, and Indigenous marginalization. Quebec's rising nationalism also challenged unity as French-speakers sought autonomy and cultural recognition.

While sharing post-war reconstruction challenges with other nations, Canada navigated them through its unique history, geography, and political culture. The boom exemplified resilience, adaptation, and balanced growth with social responsibility, leaving a defining legacy shaping Canada's identity and aspirations today.

Defining 'Good Government' in a Post-War

Context

After World War II, what did Canadians envision when they spoke of "good government"? This phrase held deep meaning and aspiration for a nation emerging from the shadows of a global conflict. But what exactly did it entail? By exploring the contours of this concept, we gain insight into the values, priorities, and dreams that shaped Canada's post-war trajectory.

At its core, "good government" in the post-war context referred to a government that actively promoted the welfare and prosperity of its citizens. It recognized its fundamental responsibility to ensure that everyone's basic needs were met—housing, healthcare, education, and employment. This was not a passive or hands-off approach to governance, but rather a proactive commitment to building a society in which everyone could thrive.

Several key elements characterized this vision of good government. First and foremost was a focus on social welfare. The post-war years saw a rapid expansion of the social safety net, with the introduction of programs like unemployment insurance, family allowances, and old-age pensions. These initiatives reflected a belief that the government had a duty to protect citizens from life's uncertainties and provide a baseline level of security and support.

Closely tied to this was a commitment to economic development and job creation. The post-war boom was fueled largely by government investments in infrastructure, industry, and technology. From constructing the Trans-Canada Highway to establishing the National Research Council, the government played a pivotal role in driving economic growth and creating opportunities for Canadians to prosper.

The roots of this conception of good government can be traced back to the early 20th century. The Great Depression exposed the limits of laissez-faire capitalism and the dire consequences of government inaction during economic crises. The war years demonstrated the power of collective action and government intervention to mobilize resources and achieve common goals.

In the post-war era, these lessons coalesced into a new vision of the government's role in society. It was no longer enough for governments to simply maintain order and enforce laws; they were now expected to actively shape the social and economic landscape, serve as a force for progress, and protect the public good.

This vision of good government faced challenges and contradictions. The rapid expansion of the state raised questions about the limits of government power and the potential for overreach. The focus on universal programs sometimes struggled to account for the diversity within the population. Additionally, the emphasis on economic growth and development occasionally clashed with emerging concerns about environmental sustainability and quality of life.

Nonetheless, the ideal of good government remained a powerful guiding force in post-war Canada. It found expression in policies and initiatives ranging from the establishment of universal healthcare to the development of the Canada Pension Plan. It shaped how Canadians viewed the role of the state and their relationship with it, contributing to a shared sense of purpose and collective responsibility that helped define the national character.

Pursuing good government in post-war Canada involved complex, ongoing negotiations among different levels of government, political parties, and social groups. It required balancing competing priorities and adapting to changing circumstances. While it was never fully realized or uncontested, it represented a noble aspiration—a vision of a society where the state served the interests of all citizens, prosperity was shared, and the common good was the highest priority.

From Victory to Vision: A Post-War Timeline

To understand how Canada built a thriving peacetime society after its wartime accomplishments, we must trace the key events, policies, and societal shifts that defined the post-war era. This timeline maps Canada's journey from 1945 onward as the nation pursued a future based on peace, order, and good government.

The roots of Canada's post-war vision began even before the war ended. In 1943, the federal government started planning the transition to a peacetime economy by establishing the Advisory Committee on Reconstruction, chaired by McGill University's principal, Cyril James. This committee recommended policies to promote full employment, social security, and economic stability after the war.

1945 marked several key events:

- World War II ended with Germany's surrender in May and Japan's in August.

- Prime Minister Mackenzie King introduced the Family Allowance program, providing monthly payments to families with children—a significant expansion of the social safety net.

- The government established the Department of Veterans Affairs to assist soldiers in reintegrating into civilian life.

1946 saw major changes:

- The Canadian Citizenship Act was passed, creating the legal concept of Canadian citizenship distinct from British subject status.

- The Central Mortgage and Housing Corporation (CMHC) was formed to address the post-war housing shortage and provide affordable housing for returning veterans and families.

- The Rand Formula, introduced through an arbitration decision by Justice Ivan Rand, mandated the automatic check-off of union dues, stabilizing labor relations.

In 1947, the Dominion-Provincial Conference on Reconstruction failed to reach an agreement on dividing taxation powers and social welfare responsibilities between the federal and provincial governments, shaping Canadian federalism in the post-war era.

1948 saw the United Nations adopt the Universal Declaration of Human Rights. Canada, under Lester B. Pearson's leadership as External Affairs Minister, played a key role in drafting this landmark document.

1949 marked Newfoundland's entry into Confederation as Canada's tenth province.

The Massey Commission began its work in 1950, examining the state of arts and culture in Canada. Its 1951 report led to the creation of the National Library of Canada and the Canada Council for the Arts.

1951 saw the passing of the Old Age Security Act, which provided universal pensions to Canadians aged 70 and over.

CBC Television began broadcasting in Montreal and Toronto in 1952, marking the beginning of the television era.

In 1956, the Canada Council for the Arts was formed to promote and fund Canadian arts and culture.

1957 brought change as John Diefenbaker's Progressive Conservatives won a minority government, ending 22 years of Liberal rule. The Gordon Commission on Canada's Economic Prospects released its final report, recommending increased investment in education, research, and resource development.

In 1958, the Diefenbaker government introduced the Agricultural Rehabilitation and Development Act (ARDA), funding rural development projects and diversifying rural economies.

The St. Lawrence Seaway opened in 1959, allowing ocean-going ships to travel from the Atlantic to the Great Lakes. This engineering marvel boosted trade and economic development.

1960 brought major developments:

- Aboriginal Canadians received the unconditional right to vote in federal elections.

- The Canadian Bill of Rights was enacted, guaranteeing certain civil liberties and freedoms as a precursor to the Charter of Rights and Freedoms.

In 1961, the National Agricultural Products Marketing Act was passed, providing a framework for national marketing boards for agricultural products.

The Trans-Canada Highway officially opened in 1962, stretching from Victoria, British Columbia, to St. John's, Newfoundland. This coast-to-coast roadway became a symbol of national unity and progress.

1965 marked major milestones:

- Canada adopted the maple leaf flag, replacing the Canadian Red Ensign. This new flag became an iconic symbol of Canadian identity.

- The Canada Pension Plan (CPP) and Quebec Pension Plan (QPP) were established, providing retirement, disability, and survivor benefits.

The Medical Care Act passed in 1966, establishing a national medicare system where the federal government shared the costs of provincial health insurance plans meeting certain criteria.

In 1967, Canada celebrated its centennial year with Expo 67 in Montreal, showcasing Canadian culture and innovation to a global audience.

This timeline highlights key milestones in Canada's post-war development but is not exhaustive. Throughout this period, Canada grappled with complex issues like Quebec nationalism, Indigenous rights, and the Cold War order. It welcomed waves of immigrants, becoming an increasingly multicultural society.

Regional differences existed in the implementation and experience of the post-war vision. The Atlantic provinces struggled with underdevelopment and outmigration, while the West experienced a resource boom. Quebec's Quiet Revolution dramatically reoriented the province's society and its relationship with the rest of Canada.

Despite challenges and variations, the overarching trajectory was one of progress and growing prosperity. Canada emerged as a middle power with a growing reputation for diplomacy and peacekeeping. It built a robust welfare state and mixed economy, providing a high standard of living for most citizens.

The post-war decades also witnessed a flourishing of Canadian culture and identity, supported by the Massey Commission, Canada Council, and CBC. Canadian literature, art, and music came into their own, reflecting and shaping the nation's sense of self.

By tracing this path from victory to vision, we gain a better understanding of the foundations of modern Canada. The post-war era's legacy continues to shape Canadian society and politics today, even as new challenges and opportunities arise. Studying this history offers insight into this vast, diverse, and constantly evolving nation's present and future.

The Foundations of Peace: Analyzing Post-War Prosperity

To truly grasp Canada's era of post-war prosperity, we must adopt an evidence-based approach. By rigorously analyzing economic data, social policies, and international relations, we can identify the key factors that drove this period of unprecedented growth and stability. This method allows us to move beyond nostalgic tales or oversimplified explanations and develop a nuanced, comprehensive understanding of this pivotal chapter in Canadian history.

The central idea is that Canada's post-war boom resulted from a combination of factors, including:

- Pent-up consumer demand and savings from the war years
- Massive government investments in infrastructure, housing, and social programs
- A rapidly expanding resource sector fueled by global demand

- The rise of new industries, such as automotive manufacturing

- High levels of immigration, which supplied labor and stimulated growth

- A stable international order and strong trade relationships, particularly with the United States

One compelling piece of evidence comes from Canada's remarkable economic data. Between 1945 and 1970, the country's Gross National Product (GNP) grew at an average annual rate of 5.5%, one of the highest rates among Western industrialized nations. Per capita income nearly tripled, rising from $1,085 in 1945 to $2,982 by 1970 (in constant 1945 dollars). This growth remained remarkably stable and sustained, with only minor recessions in the 1950s and 1960s.

A closer examination reveals nuances across sectors. Manufacturing led the charge, expanding at an annual rate of 6.5% between 1945 and 1970. The rise of the automotive industry, spurred by the 1965 Canada-U.S. Auto Pact, played a major role. By 1970, Canada was producing over 1 million vehicles annually, up from just 188,000 in 1945.

The resource sector also experienced massive growth. Crude oil production soared from 21 million barrels in 1946 to over 530 million by 1970. Natural gas production rose from 3.6 billion cubic feet in 1946 to 989.4 billion by 1970. This boom fueled related industries and infrastructure development.

However, growth was not evenly distributed across regions and sectors. The Atlantic provinces continued to struggle with underdevelopment and outmigration. The agricultural sector faced challenges as well, with farm numbers declining even as productivity increased amidst the economic shift towards manufacturing and services.

Despite these disparities, the overarching trend pointed toward expansion and improved living standards. This progress is evident in indicators such as housing starts, which averaged over 150,000 units annually in the 1950s and 1960s. Automobile ownership also grew rapidly, from one car per 16 Canadians in 1945 to one per 2.6 by 1970.

Government policies facilitated and shaped this growth through massive infrastructure investments in highways, airports, and the St. Lawrence Seaway. The creation of the Central Mortgage and Housing Corporation (CMHC) in 1946 financed the housing boom. The development of the welfare state, with initiatives like family allowances, old age pensions, and medicare, provided a safety net and stimulated consumer spending.

Internationally, Canada benefited from a stable global order and strong trade relationships under the General Agreement on Tariffs and Trade (GATT) and later the Auto Pact with the U.S. The country played an active role in shaping the post-war order through organizations such as the United Nations (UN) and the North Atlantic Treaty Organization (NATO).

Immigration also drove growth, with over 3 million newcomers arriving between 1946 and 1970. This influx supplied labor and stimulated economic activity through their spending and investment. It also transformed Canada into the multicultural society it is today.

Beyond economics, this period saw major social advancements, including the expansion of the welfare state, improved access to education and healthcare, and the beginnings of the women's and Indigenous rights movements. Canadian culture and identity flourished, bolstered by literature, art, the Canadian Broadcasting Corporation (CBC), and the Canada Council for the Arts.

Of course, historical analysis involves complexities and critiques. Some argue that the seeds of later economic challenges, such as the stagflation of the 1970s, were planted during these boom years. Others highlight persistent social inequities and the marginalization of certain groups, such as Indigenous peoples, despite overall prosperity.

Nevertheless, evidence suggests that the post-war era was pivotal and largely positive for Canada's development. It demonstrated how favorable global conditions, strategic government investment, and prudent economic policies could sustain growth and improve living standards.

Understanding this period holds relevance beyond historical curiosity. Many structures and policies shaping today's Canada emerged in that era. Studying this history offers valuable lessons as we tackle contemporary challenges like economic restructuring, social policy reform, and Canada's role in a globalizing world.

Chapter 11: The Quiet Revolution to the Charter of Rights and Freedoms

Awakening Giants: What Sparked the Quiet Revolution?

This question gets to the heart of one of the most profound transformations in Canadian history. The Quiet Revolution fundamentally altered Quebec's social, political, and cultural landscape in the 1960s. Understanding the catalysts behind this seismic shift is crucial for grasping the complexities of modern Canada.

The Quiet Revolution did not happen in a single event. It culminated long-simmering tensions and a growing desire for change among French-Canadians. For decades, the Catholic Church and conservative political elites tightly controlled Quebec. They sought to preserve traditional values and maintain the status quo. This system, known as the "Great Darkness," stifled progress. Many Quebecers felt disenfranchised and disconnected from the rest of Canada.

But beneath the surface, a new generation was emerging. They were educated, ambitious, and eager to break free from the past's shackles. These young Quebecers questioned the established order, influenced by global social justice and self-determination movements. They demanded a greater say in shaping their destiny.

At the same time, rapid industrialization and urbanization brought economic opportunities to Quebec. But it also highlighted stark inequalities between French and English-speaking Canadians. Many Francophones felt marginalized in their own province, with limited access to higher education, professional opportunities, and political power.

These simmering frustrations came to a head in the late 1950s and early 1960s. A series of events and personalities sparked the Quiet

Revolution. Premier Maurice Duplessis's death in 1959 marked an era's end. It opened the door for a new generation of leaders like Jean Lesage and René Lévesque, determined to modernize Quebec and assert its distinct identity.

Lesage's Liberal government election in 1960 was a turning point. They embarked on ambitious reforms to secularize education, nationalize key industries, and expand the state's role in social welfare. These "Lesage Reforms" laid the groundwork for a more assertive and self-confident Quebec.

But the Quiet Revolution was not solely a top-down process driven by political elites. It was a grassroots movement that drew strength from ordinary Quebecers' aspirations and activism. Students, workers, artists, and intellectuals pushed for change and redefined what it meant to be French-Canadian.

One significant development was the rise of Quebec nationalism and the push for greater autonomy within Canada. Lévesque, who founded the Parti Québécois in 1968, argued that only sovereignty could fully realize Quebec's potential and protect its distinct language, culture, and identity.

This nationalist awakening faced challenges and controversies. In 1970, the October Crisis saw the kidnapping and murder of a Quebec cabinet minister by the radical FLQ. It highlighted the potential for violence and extremism in pursuing political goals. It also tested Canada's commitment to unity and forced a national reckoning on Quebec's place within the federation.

Ultimately, the Quiet Revolution transformed Quebec from a traditional, church-dominated society into a modern, secular, and assertive nation within Canada. It unleashed powerful forces of change that continue shaping the country today, from the ongoing debate over Quebec sovereignty to the push for greater provincial autonomy and distinct cultural identities' recognition.

Redefining Rights: The Birth of the Charter

The Charter of Rights and Freedoms marks a landmark achievement in Canadian history. It boldly declares the fundamental rights and freedoms that define our nation. To truly appreciate its significance, we must understand the historical journey leading to its creation - from the earliest calls for constitutional rights to the passionate debates that gave birth to this transformative document.

The roots trace back to the aftermath of World War II when the world awakened to the horrors of totalitarianism and the importance of individual rights. In 1947, Saskatchewan passed Canada's first bill of rights, prohibiting discrimination based on race, religion, and origin. This pioneering law by Premier Tommy Douglas set a precedent for protecting human rights.

Over the following decades, calls for a national bill intensified, driven by Canadians' desire to enshrine cherished freedoms. Prime Minister John Diefenbaker responded in 1960 with the Canadian Bill of Rights, recognizing certain rights and freedoms. While groundbreaking, this Bill had limitations as a federal statute without constitutional status.

The 1960s and 70s saw growing momentum for an entrenched charter fueled by social upheavals. Quebec's Quiet Revolution, the women's and Indigenous movements, and diversity concerns heightened awareness about stronger rights protections.

A pivotal moment arrived in 1980 after the narrow defeat of Quebec's sovereignty referendum. Prime Minister Pierre Trudeau embarked on repatriating the Constitution and enshrining a charter of rights and freedoms. He envisioned the Charter uniting Canadians around shared values and protecting minority rights.

Achieving this vision wasn't easy. Trudeau faced opposition from some provinces fearing infringement on their powers. Intense negotiations led to compromises like the notwithstanding clause allowing provincial overrides. But the Charter prevailed, adopted in 1982's Constitution Act.

The Charter entrenched a wide range of rights and freedoms: expression, religion, democratic rights, mobility, legal rights, equality, prohibiting discrimination by race, origin, color, religion, sex, age, or disability. It recognized Canada's multicultural heritage and Indigenous peoples' rights.

Voices of Change: Key Figures of the Era

Canada was shaped by visionary leaders in the era before the Charter of Rights and Freedoms. These pioneers fearlessly advocated for change. Their bold actions and commitment to justice laid the foundation for the rights and freedoms we cherish today. Let's look at the lives of these remarkable individuals whose legacy continues to inspire:

1. Tommy Douglas pioneered the Saskatchewan Bill of Rights and was the father of Medicare.
2. Pierre Trudeau was the charismatic prime minister who brought home the Constitution and championed the Charter.
3. Thérèse Casgrain was a feminist icon who tirelessly fought for women's rights and social justice.
4. Frank Arthur Calder paved the way for recognizing Aboriginal rights as an Indigenous leader.

5. Jean Lesage was the Quebec premier whose Quiet Revolution transformed the province and ignited calls for change.

As Saskatchewan's premier, Tommy Douglas ignited the spark for protecting human rights in Canada. In 1947, his government passed the groundbreaking Saskatchewan Bill of Rights. It prohibited discrimination based on race, religion, and origin. This landmark law set a precedent for protecting individual rights. It inspired other provinces to follow. Douglas vocally advocated for a national bill of rights beyond Saskatchewan. His legacy as Medicare's father and a champion of equality continues shaping Canada's values.

Prime Minister Pierre Trudeau took centre stage in battling for constitutional reform and entrenching the Charter. With his sharp intellect and fierce determination, Trudeau navigated complex politics to patriate the Constitution. He enshrined fundamental rights and freedoms despite opposition. Trudeau passionately defended individual liberties. His commitment to building a just society left an indelible mark on Canada's identity.

The indomitable Thérèse Casgrain dedicated her life to pursuing women's rights and social justice. As a Quebec suffragette leader, she fearlessly challenged the status quo. Casgrain fought for women's right to vote. Her tireless advocacy extended beyond the ballot box. She championed pay equity, family planning, and women's education access. Casgrain's courage and pursuit of equality helped pave the way for gender equality in the Charter.

Frank Arthur Calder played a pivotal role in asserting Aboriginal rights as an Indigenous leader. He was the first Indigenous person elected to a Canadian legislature. Calder advocated for First Nations rights and interests. His landmark Calder v. British Columbia case laid the groundwork for recognizing Aboriginal title and treaty rights in the Constitution. Calder determinedly asserted Indigenous sovereignty and protected traditional lands. This shaped the Charter's acknowledgment of existing Aboriginal and treaty rights.

Quebec Premier Jean Lesage ushered in the Quiet Revolution – a period of profound social and political change. Under his leadership, Quebec modernized, secularized, and asserted its distinct identity. Lesage's ambitious reforms transformed education, healthcare, and the economy. They ignited desire for greater autonomy. His government's push for its own Charter of Rights and Freedoms set the stage for larger constitutional debates shaping the nation's future.

Through courage, conviction, and tireless advocacy, these leaders laid the groundwork for the Charter of Rights and Freedoms. Their vision of an equal, just Canada based on individual liberties inspired dreams of a better future. Their legacy reminds us of leadership's power to create change and the importance of standing up for our beliefs.

The Charter's journey was not easy. It required countless individuals daring to challenge the status quo and fight for a just society. From grassroots activists to legal scholars, Indigenous leaders to women's rights advocates – each played a vital role shaping the discourse and pushing change.

The Federalism Debate: Unity Vs. Autonomy

In the heart of Canada's constitutional landscape lies a profound tension – the delicate balance between national unity and provincial autonomy. This debate has shaped the very fabric of the nation, pitting the desire for a strong, cohesive federation against the yearning for regional self-determination and cultural preservation. Nowhere is this tension more palpable than in the enduring question of Quebec's place within Canada.

The roots of this federalism debate run deep, intertwined with Canada's colonial history, linguistic duality, and the evolving aspirations of its diverse regions. It is a debate that has both united and divided, forcing Canadians to confront fundamental questions about the nature of their federation and the distribution of powers between the central government and the provinces.

At the core of this debate are two competing visions of Canada. On one side, proponents of a strong central government argue that national unity and equality require a robust federal presence. They believe in setting national standards, redistributing wealth, and ensuring that all Canadians have access to comparable services and opportunities, regardless of where they live. They contend that without a strong central government, Canada risks fragmentation and the erosion of its shared values and identity.

On the other side, advocates of greater provincial autonomy assert that Canada's diversity is best served by a decentralized federation. They argue that provinces are best positioned to respond to the unique challenges and aspirations of their populations. An overly centralized federation, they say, risks stifling innovation, imposing one-size-fits-all solutions, and fueling resentment and alienation.

Nowhere has this debate been more fierce than in the case of Quebec. As a predominantly French-speaking province with a distinct cultural heritage, Quebec has long sought recognition of its unique status within Canada. From the Quiet Revolution of the 1960s to the referendums on sovereignty in 1980 and 1995, Quebec's quest for greater autonomy and recognition has been a defining feature of Canadian federalism.

Central to Quebec's demands has been the concept of *asymmetrical federalism* – the idea that Quebec should have powers and responsibilities different from those of other provinces in areas critical to its distinct identity, such as language, culture, and immigration. This has been met with both understanding and resistance from other parts of Canada, with some fearing that asymmetry could lead to a patchwork federation and undermine national cohesion.

The patriation of the Constitution in 1982 and the entrenchment of the Charter of Rights and Freedoms brought these tensions to a head. While the Charter was hailed by many as a landmark achievement, enshrining fundamental rights and freedoms for all Canadians, Quebec viewed it with suspicion, fearing that it could be used to undermine its language laws and distinct status.

Quebec's refusal to sign the Constitution Act of 1982 led to years of constitutional negotiations aimed at bringing Quebec back into the constitutional fold. The Meech Lake Accord of 1987 and the Charlottetown Accord of 1992 both included provisions recognizing

Quebec as a distinct society and granting it greater autonomy in certain areas. However, the failure of both accords to secure national ratification left the question of Quebec's place in Canada unresolved and the wounds of the federalism debate raw.

In the years since, the federalism debate has continued to evolve. Successive federal and provincial governments have sought to find a balance between unity and autonomy, centralization and decentralization. The 2006 motion recognizing Quebec as a nation within Canada was seen by some as a step towards reconciliation, while others viewed it as a purely symbolic gesture.

Beyond Quebec, the federalism debate has also been shaped by the evolving roles and aspirations of other provinces. Western alienation, driven by a sense that the federal government is unresponsive to the needs and interests of the West, has fueled calls for greater provincial control over resources and economic development. Indigenous self-government and the recognition of Indigenous rights have added another dimension to the debate, challenging traditional notions of Canadian federalism.

Challenging the Status Quo: The Charter's Impact on Society

The examination of the *Charter of Rights and Freedoms* and its profound influence on Canadian society is not just a recount of historical events; it's a dive into the very fabric that constructs Canadian identity and governance. Through an evidence-based approach, this analysis aims to unravel how the introduction of the Charter revolutionized civil liberties and reshaped the relationship between the government and the governed in Canada. Focusing on empirical evidence, this method ensures a grounded and unbiased exploration of the Charter's tangible impacts, scrutinizing key legal battles, landmark rulings, and the living nature of this document.

The main proposition at hand is the assertion that the *Charter of Rights and Freedoms* has fundamentally altered the landscape of Canadian society by enhancing civil liberties and transforming governmental responsibilities. This not only involves the protection of individual rights but also the accountability of governmental actions in the face of those rights.

The main piece of evidence supporting this claim emerges from a series of key legal battles and landmark rulings in the Supreme Court of Canada. The analysis begins with the striking down of laws that infringed upon rights guaranteed by the Charter, a pivotal move that set precedent for future legal interpretations and governmental legislation. One prominent example is the 1988 case *R v. Oakes*, which established the **Oakes test**, a critical framework for determining whether a law can justifiably infringe on Charter rights. This case underscores the Charter's capacity to challenge existing laws and set new legal standards.

Delving deeper into this evidence, the **Oakes test** involves examining the objective of the law that limits a Charter right, ensuring it is sufficiently important and that the means of limiting the right are reasonable and justifiable. The credibility of this methodology arises from its rigorous application and its origin from the highest court in the country, providing a solid foundation for evaluating the Charter's impact on legislative action.

Despite the Charter's apparent success in enhancing civil liberties, there exists counter-evidence suggesting limitations in its application. Critics argue that the Charter has, at times, failed to protect the rights of the most vulnerable communities in Canada, pointing out disparities in the enforcement and interpretation of its provisions. This challenge introduces a complexity to the analysis, pressing the need for a balanced perspective.

Echoes of Revolution: The Quiet Revolution's

Lasting Legacy

The Quiet Revolution, though silent, sent shockwaves through the fabric of Canadian society. It transformed not just the face of Quebec, but also set a precedent for change across the entire nation. But what makes this period so remarkable? What is its lasting legacy that continues to echo through the corridors of Canadian identity, politics, and society today?

At its core, the Quiet Revolution was a period of intense socio-political and cultural change in Quebec during the 1960s. It was akin to a butterfly emerging from its chrysalis: Quebec transformed from a conservative, religious province into a secular, progressive society. This metamorphosis was not just about changing governments or policies; it was about altering the very heartbeat of a society. Imagine a landscape where the once immovable mountains of tradition and conservatism begin to dance — that was the magic of the Quiet Revolution.

Key elements of this transformative era include the secularization of the state, the vast expansion of the welfare system, and the assertion of Quebec's right to self-determination. Each component, like threads in a tapestry, wove together to redefine Quebec's place within Canada and the world. The secularization of the state distanced public policy from Church influence, allowing for a more inclusive governance that reflected a diverse society. Expanding the welfare system showed a commitment to social justice and equity, ensuring that the safety net Canadians pride themselves on became stronger and more reliable. Asserting the right to self-determination ignited a fire of nationalism that would shape Quebec's political discourse for decades.

Tracing its origins back to the quiet stirrings of discontent in post-World War II Quebec, the Quiet Revolution was a response to the growing desire for change among Quebecers. Fueled by a collective yearning for modernization and a break from the shackles of provincialism, this period was both an uprising and an awakening. It was a revolution that didn't need the clamor of battle to announce its arrival; it came on the whispers of revolutionaries who dreamt of a different Quebec.

The significance of the Quiet Revolution transcends its historical moment, weaving its legacy into the broad tapestry of Canadian identity. It reminded Canada of the power of silent transformations and the importance of cultural and political autonomy. This era wasn't just about changing laws or governance structures; it was about reimagining what Canadian society could be — more inclusive, more progressive, and more reflective of its diverse population.

In modern-day Canada, the spirit of the Quiet Revolution manifests in ongoing debates about rights, autonomy, and identity. The shift towards valuing multiculturalism and bilingualism nationwide can be traced back to the revolutions' assertion of French-Canadian identity. The Quiet Revolution set the stage for conversations about federalism, cultural pluralism, and indigenous rights that continue to shape Canadian policy and society.

At its essence, the legacy of the Quiet Revolution challenges us to consider how silent transformations can lead to profound societal shifts. It is a testament to the strength of quiet, steady change over the bombastic noise of conflict. In the currents of contemporary Canadian dialogues—about everything from environmental policy to technology and privacy—the echoes of the Quiet Revolution remind us that at the heart of every debate, every policy change, and every societal shift, is the fundamental quest for a just, equitable, and free society. It prompts us to look beyond the loud and the dramatic, to find the powerful currents of change that flow in the quiet.

Chapter 12: A Global Player

Silicon Valley North: The Tech Boom and Canada's Future

The fabric of Canada's burgeoning tech scene, affectionately termed *'Silicon Valley North,'* is woven from the threads of multiculturalism, inclusivity, and resilience. It's not just the cold weather or the breathtaking landscapes that define this northern powerhouse. It's the vibrant and diverse ecosystem that fosters groundbreaking innovation and technological breakthroughs. But how does this all come to play in the world of tech, where competition is fierce, and the race for the next big thing is relentless?

Within the heart of cities like Toronto, Vancouver, and Montreal, a new narrative is unfolding. These cities aren't just geographical markers; they're linchpins in Canada's tech expansion, each contributing its unique flavor to the mix. Toronto, with its bustling urban landscape, offers a melting pot of cultures and ideas—a fertile ground for startups and tech giants alike. Vancouver, with its scenic beauty and strategic location, bridges the gap between the North American tech scene and the booming markets of Asia. Montreal, with its historic charm and cultural richness, has emerged as a powerhouse of AI research and innovation. Together, these cities sketch the contours of *'Silicon Valley North.'* But who are the maestros orchestrating this symphony?

The main actors in this unfolding drama include visionary entrepreneurs who see beyond the horizon, astute investors who fuel the dreams of tomorrow, and, perhaps most pivotally, the Canadian people. Their diverse backgrounds and perspectives are the bedrock of innovation. Behind each startup success story and each technological breakthrough, there's a team that mirrors the mosaic of modern

Canada. It is this diversity that drives creativity, problem-solving, and resilience against the ever-present winds of change.

The challenge, however, isn't trivial. To compete on the world stage and sustain its explosive growth, *'Silicon Valley North'* must navigate the global tech landscape while remaining true to Canadian values—a juggling act of high stakes. How does one cultivate a world-class tech ecosystem under these conditions? The approach is multifaceted, underpinned by policies that promote investment in tech, education that prepares the next generation of innovators, and initiatives that support the integration of international talent with Canadian values at its core.

Strategies are as varied as they are innovative. Government incentives for tech startups, tax breaks for investors, and collaborations between universities and the private sector to innovate on the cutting edge. Yet, it isn't just about the financial or infrastructural support. Canada's tech boom is as much about fostering an inclusive, welcoming environment for talent from around the globe as it is about the technological advancements themselves. This ethos is what attracts, retains, and nurtures the human capital necessary to fuel continuous innovation. It's a testament to the idea that the future is built together, not in isolation.

The outcomes of these efforts are tangible and promising. Employment rates within the tech sector have soared, with thousands of jobs being created every year. Startups have flourished, scaling from local operations to global contenders. Canada's GDP has seen a healthy uptick, attributed in no small part to the tech industry's explosive growth. These successes paint a picture of a thriving ecosystem that competes not by racing to the bottom but by continuously elevating its collective capabilities.

From this vantage, what lessons can be gleaned? The narrative of *'Silicon Valley North'* serves as a compelling case study for the world. It exemplifies how diversity and inclusivity aren't just ethical imperatives but strategic advantages. By juxtaposing Canada's approach with more insular models, one appreciates the robustness of a tech ecosystem rooted in a variety of perspectives and experiences. Criticisms remain, as with any ambitious undertaking. Debates about the sustainability of rapid growth, concerns over housing and infrastructure, and the ever-present specter of inequality pose significant questions. Yet, these challenges are met not with complacency but with the resolve to innovate and improve.

In tying back to the overarching theme of our exploration, *'Silicon Valley North'* is more than a nickname or a geographical reference. It's a microcosm of Canada's future in the global order, a testament to the idea that the strength of a nation, especially in the realm of technology, lies in its ability to embrace diversity, foster inclusivity, and build resilience. As this chapter of Canada's tech journey continues to unfold, it does so not as a solo act but as a chorus, with each voice adding depth, nuance, and beauty to the story.

Thus, as we marvel at the skyscrapers and the digital infrastructures, let us not forget the foundation upon which they stand: a commitment to a society where innovation is fueled by diversity, driven by inclusivity, and made resilient through unity. *'Silicon Valley North'* is not just Canada's tech story; it is a beacon for the world, illuminating a path where progress and values walk hand in hand.

From Past to Present: Canada's Journey to Global Influence

Imagine the world as a vast, intricate mosaic, with each nation a unique piece contributing to the grand design. Canada, in this global mosaic, has become known for its role as a peacemaker and advocate for justice, stitching together fragments of peace and harmony with the threads of diplomacy and understanding. But how did this come to be? The journey from past to present, from a relatively unknown entity to a nation with a commanding presence on the international stage, is a testament to the power of steadfast principles and visionary leadership.

Earliest Influences:

The seed of what would bloom into Canada's influential role on the world stage was planted in the early days of confederation, in 1867. This was a time when the concept of a unified, peace-oriented Canada began to take shape, influenced by its foundational values of diversity, dialogue, and mutual respect. These values, deeply rooted in the Canadian ethos, would come to define its approach to global engagement.

Pivotal Moments:

- **1919:** Canada's independent signature on the Treaty of Versailles marked its first separate international agreement from Britain. This symbolized the country's emerging autonomy and influence.

- **1956:** During the Suez Crisis, Lester B. Pearson played a pivotal role in establishing the United Nations Emergency Force, highlighting Canada's commitment to global peacekeeping.

- **1987:** Canada led the Montreal Protocol on substances that deplete the ozone layer, showcasing its dedication to addressing global environmental challenges.

- **1995:** The establishment of the Canadian International Development Agency (CIDA) reflected Canada's commitment to international development and poverty reduction.

Cultural and Regional Adaptations:

Canadian diplomacy has always been characterized by its chameleon-like ability to adapt, listening intently to the needs and concerns of different cultures and regions. Whether through peacekeeping missions in war-torn countries or facilitating dialogues in conflict zones, Canada has displayed an uncanny ability to understand diverse perspectives. This adaptability is not about losing one's identity but about enhancing global cooperation through empathy and respect.

Contemporary Practice and Innovations:

In the digital age, Canadian diplomacy has embraced technology to further its reach and impact. From leading digital rights initiatives to leveraging social media for diplomatic dialogue, Canada has innovated its approach to keep pace with changing times. These contemporary practices have ensured that Canadian diplomacy remains relevant, effective, and deeply interconnected with global citizens' daily lives.

Challenges on the Horizon:

Yet, the path of diplomacy is strewn with challenges. In an era of rising nationalism and global tensions, Canadian diplomacy faces tests like never before. Issues such as climate change, cyber security, and global health crises demand a recalibration of strategies. But within these challenges lie opportunities—for dialogue, for innovation, and for reaffirming Canada's role as a beacon of hope and leadership on the world stage.

Diplomatic Milestones:

As with any journey, there are milestones that serve as beacons, illuminating the path forward. The Ottawa Treaty, prohibiting landmines; Canada's proactive stance on the Syrian refugee crisis—all are testament to what diplomacy, guided by core values and courage, can achieve. These milestones are not just achievements but signposts, indicating the ongoing evolution of Canadian influence in the arena of global diplomacy.

The essence of Canadian diplomacy, woven through the fabric of its history, is a narrative of peace, perseverance, and the pursuit of a fairer, more inclusive world. Each chapter of Canada's journey on the international stage builds on the last, a continuum that speaks to the enduring power of diplomacy when anchored in the deep-rooted values of dialogue, diversity, and respect for human rights. As the world changes, so too does the landscape of global diplomacy, but the principles that define Canada's approach remain as relevant and revolutionary as ever.

Pioneering Peacekeeping: Canada's Legacy and Lessons Learned

Delving into Canada's legacy in peacekeeping is like wandering through a garden of contrasts. It's a tale of triumphs blooming amidst challenges, and above all, it's a testament to the nation's heartfelt commitment to nurturing global peace and security. This journey not only highlights Canada's peacekeeping efforts but also reveals the hard-won lessons and lasting impressions these endeavors have left on the world stage.

The landscape of Canada's peacekeeping legacy is marked by:

Groundbreaking Initiatives in Peacekeeping Missions

Canada's peacekeeping journey is sprinkled with pioneering initiatives, each shining like a beacon of the country's innovative approach to resolving conflicts. The Suez Crisis of 1956 is a monumental chapter. Here, Canada proposed a peacekeeping force to ensure the withdrawal of invaders, setting a global precedent. This bold move not only calmed potential escalation but also shaped the very essence of peacekeeping. It introduced a new way of thinking in international diplomacy. Canada's audacity to propose a non-combative, multinational force to manage conflicts carved out a special place for the nation in the history of peacemaking.

Confrontation with Operational Challenges

The path of peacekeeping is filled with complexities, and Canada's journey is no different. The harsh terrain of operational challenges, from logistical nightmares to the unpredictable nature of conflict zones, posed formidable barriers. Yet, it was within these fiery crucibles that Canada's resilience shone brightly. They forged strategies and tactics that would guide future missions. The engagement in Somalia, for example, exposed the difficulties of operating in a lawless land. It led to the grim realization that peacekeepers themselves could falter and become perpetrators. This dark chapter forced a reckoning within the Canadian forces, spurring reforms in training, conduct, and engagement rules.

Impacts on Military and Diplomatic Policies

The echoes of Canada's peacekeeping efforts have resonated through its military and diplomatic corridors, shaping policies and agendas. The shift from traditional peacekeeping to peace enforcement missions required a recalibration of military training. This new approach prioritized cultural sensitivity, negotiation skills, and a deep understanding of complex geopolitical landscapes. Diplomatically, Canada's commitment to global peace translated into a proactive stance on international platforms. They advocated for robust peacekeeping frameworks and championed the cause of conflict prevention. This dual approach highlighted Canada's recognition of the delicate balance between military readiness and diplomatic finesse.

Emerging Complexities in Modern Peacekeeping Efforts

As the world spins into an era marked by increasingly intricate conflicts, the terrain of peacekeeping has transformed into a labyrinth of political, religious, and ethnic intricacies. Canada's engagement in modern peacekeeping operations reflects a nuanced understanding of these complexities. From the hybrid UN-AU mission in Darfur to its advisory roles in rebuilding war-torn societies, each mission is a mosaic of triumphs and trials. These experiences have contributed to a reservoir of knowledge on navigating the gaps between peacekeeping ideals and the gritty realities on the ground.

The tapestry of Canada's peacekeeping legacy, woven with threads of ambition and introspection, highlights a journey marked by an unwavering commitment to global peace and a humbling recognition of the challenges that journey entails. This saga of pioneering spirit, operational resilience, policy evolution, and adaptation to emerging complexities offers invaluable insights into the essence and demands of peacekeeping in our world today. It paints a picture of a nation that, despite facing the tumultuous waves of geopolitical strife, remains anchored by its peacekeeping ethos.

Afterword

As we reach the end of this exploration into the rich and multifaceted history of Canada, I want to extend my deepest gratitude to you, the reader, for embarking on this journey with me. From the early days of Indigenous cultures to the modern era of global influence, we've navigated through centuries of growth, challenges, and transformation that have shaped this remarkable nation.

Writing about Canada's history has been both a privilege and a profound learning experience. The stories of resilience, innovation, and collaboration that weave together Canada's past and present are truly inspiring. It is my hope that this book has provided you with a deeper understanding of how diverse threads of culture, history, and identity have come together to form the fabric of Canada.

If you found value in this book and enjoyed the journey through Canada's historical landscape, I would be incredibly grateful if you could take a moment to leave a rating or review. Your feedback not only helps me as an author but also assists future readers in discovering and appreciating the story of Canada. Reviews are essential in guiding others towards meaningful reads and sharing the narrative that continues to evolve.

Thank you once again for your time and engagement. Your interest in Canada's history enriches the dialogue about this nation's past and future. I hope that this book has sparked curiosity and encouraged a greater appreciation for the diverse and dynamic elements that make up Canada's heritage.

Warmest regards,

History Nerds

References:

Berton, P. 1971. *The Last Spike: The Great Railway 1881-1885.* McClelland and Stewart.

Bothwell, R. 1999. *The History of Canada.* University of Toronto Press.

Li, P. 1988. "*Chinese Laborers and the Building of the Canadian Pacific Railway.*" Journal of Canadian Studies, 23(4).

Pentland, H. C. 1970. *Labour and Capital in Canada 1650-1860.* University of Toronto Press.

Shields, D. S. 2015. *The Seven Years' War: A Transatlantic History.* Cambridge University Press.

Borneman, W. R. 2006. *The French and Indian War: Deciding the Fate of North America.* HarperCollins.

Don't miss out!

Visit the website below and you can sign up to receive emails whenever History Nerds publishes a new book. There's no charge and no obligation.

https://books2read.com/r/B-A-ODOK-PPBXE

BOOKS 2 READ

Connecting independent readers to independent writers.

Also by History Nerds

Ancient Empires
The Ottoman Empire
Rome: The Rise and Fall
The Mongol Empire
The Assyrian Empire
Ancient Egypt

Celtic Heroes and Legends
Celtic History
William Butler Yeats: Nobel Prize Winning Poet
Robert the Bruce
Scáthach
Finn McCool
William Wallace: Scotland's Great Freedom Fighter

Frauen des Krieges
Boudica: Königin der Icener
Jeanne d'Arc
Irena Sendler
Virginia Hall

Königin Amanirenas
Anne Frank
Florence Nightingale
Nakano Takeko
Lyudmila Pawlitschenko
Lagertha

Geschichte der welt
Die Geschichte Schottlands
Die Geschichte von Wales

Great Wars of the World
World War 1
World War 2
The Napoleonic Wars: One Shot at Glory
The Serbian Revolution: 1804-1835
Peace Won by the Saber: The Crimean War, 1853-1856
The American Civil War

Pirate Chronicles
Grace O'Malley: The Pirate Queen of Ireland
Blackbeard
William Kidd
Ching Shih
Anne Bonny

The History of England
Roman Britain
Medieval England
The Wars of the Roses
Tudor England

The History of the Vikings
Vikings
Longships on Restless Seas

Women of War
Boudica: Queen of the Iceni
Joan of Arc
Irena Sendler
Virginia Hall
Queen Amanirenas
Anne Frank
Florence Nightingale
Nakano Takeko
Lyudmila Pavlichenko
Lagertha
Women of War Omnibus: Books 1-5
Women of War Omnibus: Books 6-10

World History
The History of the United Kingdom

The History of Ireland
The History of America
The History of Scotland
The History of Wales
The History of India
The History of Canada

Standalone
Grace O'Malley: Die Piratenkönigin von Irland

www.ingramcontent.com/pod-product-compliance
Lightning Source LLC
Chambersburg PA
CBHW062142150726
47991CB00006B/2152